BASEBALL AMERICA PRESENTS

BEFORE
THEY WERE
STARS

BASEBALL AMERICA INC. · DURHAM, N.C.

BaseBall america

ESTABLISHED 1981

P.O. BOX 12877, DURHAM, NC 27709 • PHONE (919) 682-9635

EDITOR AND PUBLISHER B.J. Schecter *@bjschecter*

EXECUTIVE EDITORS J.J. Cooper *@jjcoop36*

Matt Eddy *@MattEddyBA*

CHIEF REVENUE OFFICER Don Hintze

DIRECTOR OF BUSINESS DEVELOPMENT Ben Leigh

EDITORIAL

ASSOCIATE EDITORS Kegan Lowe *@KeganLowe*

Josh Norris *@jnorris427*

SENIOR WRITER Ben Badler *@benbadler*

NATIONAL WRITERS Teddy Cahill *@tedcahill*

Carlos Collazo *@CarlosACollazo*

Kyle Glaser *@KyleAGlaser*

Michael Lananna *@mlananna*

WEB EDITOR Mark Chiarelli *@Mark_Chiarelli*

SPECIAL CONTRIBUTOR Tim Newcomb *@tdnewcomb*

PRODUCTION

DESIGN & PRODUCTION DIRECTOR Sara Hiatt McDaniel

MULTIMEDIA MANAGER Linwood Webb

DESIGN ASSISTANT James Alworth

BUSINESS

TECHNOLOGY MANAGER Brent Lewis

ACCOUNT EXECUTIVE Kellen Coleman

OFFICE MANAGER AND CUSTOMER SERVICE Angela Lewis

CUSTOMER SERVICE Jonathan Smith

STATISTICAL SERVICE

MAJOR LEAGUE BASEBALL ADVANCED MEDIA

Alliance
>>>> BASEBALL <<<<

BASEBALL AMERICA ENTERPRISES

CHAIRMAN & CEO Gary Green

PRESIDENT Larry Botel

GENERAL COUNSEL Matthew Pace

DIRECTOR OF MARKETING Amy Heart

INVESTOR RELATIONS Michele Balfour

DIRECTOR OF OPERATIONS Joan Disalvo

PARTNERS Jon Ashley

Stephen Alepa

Martie Cordaro

Brian Rothschild

Andrew Fox

Maurice Haroche

Dan Waldman

Sonny Kalsi

Glenn Isaacson

Robert Hernreich

Craig Amazeen

Peter Ruprecht

Beryl Snyder

Tom Steiglehner

3STƎP

MANAGING PARTNER David Geaslen

CHIEF CONTENT OFFICER Jonathan Segal

CHIEF FINANCIAL OFFICER Sue Murphy

DIRECTOR OF DIGITAL CONTENT Tom Johnson

BASEBALL AMERICA (ISSN 0745-5372/USPS 591-210) is published bi-weekly with a double issue in August and December, 24 issues per year, by Baseball America Enterprises, LLC, 4319 South Alston Ave, Suite 103, Durham, NC 27713. Subscription rate is $92.95 for one year; Canada $118.95 (U.S. funds); all other foreign $144.95 per year (U.S. funds). Periodicals postage paid at Durham, NC, & additional mailing offices. Occasionally our subscriber list is made available to reputable firms offering goods and services we believe would be of interest to our readers. If you prefer to be excluded, please send your current address label and a note requesting to be excluded from these promotions to Baseball America Enterprises, LLC, 4319 South Alston Ave, Suite 103, Durham, NC 27713, Attn Privacy Coordinator.

©2018 by Baseball America Enterprises, LLC. All Rights Reserved. Printed in the USA.

BASEBALL AMERICA PRESENTS

BEFORE THEY WERE STARS

Editors
Matt Eddy, Kegan Lowe and J.J. Cooper

Contributing Editors
Chris Hilburn-Trenkle, Michael Magnuson

Database and Application Development
Brent Lewis

Design & Production
James Alworth, Sara Hiatt McDaniel, Linwood Webb

Programming & Technical Development
Brent Lewis

Cover Photos
MAIN PHOTO: Derek Jeter at Yankee Stadium,
Sept. 25, 2014.
Photo by Jim McIsaac/Getty Images.

INSET: Derek Jeter poses prior to a game circa 1992.
Photo by Focus on Sport/Getty Images.

For additional copies, visit our Website at
BaseballAmerica.com or call 1-800-845-2726 to order.

US $34.95 / CAN $46.95, plus shipping
and handling per order. Expedited shipping available.

Distributed by Simon & Schuster.
ISBN-13: 978-1-932391-75-6

Statistics provided by Major League Baseball Advanced
Media and Compiled by Baseball America.

ABOUT THE BOOK

We now live in a world of widespread prospect awareness.

Vladimir Guerrero Jr. has yet to play an official game for the Blue Jays, but he's already more famous than two-thirds of players on the Blue Jays' big league roster. Cubs fans counted down the days until Kris Bryant became the team's third baseman.

But that wasn't always the case. Besides the occasional spring training sighting, prospects existed in the often-forgotten world of the minor leagues. There were the major leagues, where big league players starred, and the minors, where everyone else worked in obscurity.

Baseball America founder Allan Simpson wanted to change that world. It was his idea to cover the minors (and amateur baseball and the draft) with a focus on picking out the stars of tomorrow long before they arrived. And so he began Baseball America magazine in 1981.

He was crazy to even try. There were no cell phones. The Internet as we know it didn't exist. Statistics came by mail every couple of weeks. Tracking down a scout or front office official meant leaving a long-distance message through voicemail and waiting—hoping—for a callback.

But he and a small group of fellow trailblazers proved that it could be done. From day one, Baseball America ranked prospects, writing scouting reports to provide insights into an area that had previously gone almost unnoticed.

And by doing so, Baseball America helped birth the world we live in today. The one where we all count the days until the next great prospect reaches the majors. Nowadays, it's a given that it's possible to spot future stars before they reach the majors. But that wasn't always the case. It took years of Simpson and his staff being proven right more often than not to get us to this point.

In those early years, many scouts and behind-the-scenes front office officials were excited that someone was paying attention. Some teams simply read their scouting reports over the phone to Simpson to help him prepare Top 10 Prospects rankings. Athletics general manager Sandy Alderson famously relied on Baseball America's Yankees Top 10 Prospects list for his 1985 Rickey Henderson trade—he just asked for the top five Yankees prospects in return.

This book is the fruit of the labor of many scouts and many reporters. Baseball America has worked for nearly 40 years to find tomorrow's stars today. Predicting prospects is extremely difficult and we've had our misses as well as our hits. But this book gives you a chance to see what was expected of the best in baseball before they were household names. Travel back to when they were simply another young player with the dream of becoming a big leaguer, before they were stars.

JJ COOPER
EXECUTIVE EDITOR, BASEBALL AMERICA

ABBREVIATIONS

ABB	LEAGUE	LEVEL
AA	American Association	Triple-A (through 1997)
IL	International	Triple-A
PCL	Pacific Coast	Triple-A
EL	Eastern	Double-A
SL	Southern	Double-A
TL	Texas	Double-A
CAL	California	High Class A
CAR	Carolina	High Class A
FSL	Florida State	High Class A

ABB	LEAGUE	LEVEL
MWL	Midwest	Low Class A
SAL	South Atlantic	Low Class A
NYP	New York-Penn	Short-season
NWL	Northwest	Short-season
APP	Appalachian	Rookie
AZL	Arizona	Rookie
GCL	Gulf Coast	Rookie
PIO	Pioneer	Rookie

A HISTORY OF BASEBALL AMERICA PROSPECT RANKINGS

A few hundred minor league prospects have matured into major league stars in the 38 years that Baseball America has been ranking prospects as comprehensively as only BA can.

Prospect rankings have been an integral part of BA from its beginnings in 1981. The October issue from that year ranks the Top 10 Prospects for all the full-season minor leagues.

The first scouting report to appear in that issue belongs to 20-year-old Phillies shortstop Julio Franco, whose age has since been revised upward by two years. Franco ranked No. 1 in the Eastern League in 1981 and was considered a "can't-miss player who someday soon will replace Larry Bowa in Philadelphia."

Among the other prospects we highlighted in that 1981 issue are current major league managers Terry Francona and Don Mattingly and current broadcasters Ron Darling and Harold Reynolds.

BA began ranking the Top 10 Prospects for each organization beginning with the 1983 season. The National League West was the first division to be featured, and future big leaguers such as Eric Davis, Ozzie Guillen, Kevin McReynolds and Mitch Williams all received reports in that issue.

Best Tools balloting was the next major prospect enhancement. It first appeared on the minor league side in 1986, when minor league managers singled out David Cone, Randy Johnson and Larry Walker as having loud tools that would impact the game.

The final prospect ranking breakthrough came in the form of the Top 100 Prospects, which was introduced in 1990 and was headlined that year by Steve Avery, Ben McDonald and John Olerud in the top three spots.

ABOUT THE PLAYER SELECTION PROCESS

Filling out the player roster for Before They Were Stars was a daunting task. Because so many minor leaguers have developed into major stars in Baseball America's nearly four decades in the prospect ranking game, I'm still not convinced I chose all the correct players to highlight in this book.

In other words, the player you are convinced got snubbed probably was considered for this book at some point.

When choosing players, I placed an emphasis on peak contributions and concentrated value, such as MVP or Cy Young Award-type seasons, All-Star Game appearances, Gold Gloves won and even Hall of Fame balloting results.

This book was never intended to capture the top 120-plus players of the past 40 years as ranked by an advanced metric such as wins above replacement. Rather, I chose to celebrate big seasons by big stars for whom BA had detailed scouting information dating back to, well, before they were stars.

That last clause disqualified a trio of rookies from the early 1980s who went on to build Hall of Fame careers. Tony Gwynn, Cal Ripken Jr. and Ryne Sandberg all appeared in the pages of BA before they established themselves in the majors, but true scouting information on the trio is scarce.

Fortunately, we had no shortage of worthy candidates to complete our roster, including 18 Hall of Famers for who you might have first received notice in the pages of Baseball America.

MATT EDDY
EXECUTIVE EDITOR, BASEBALL AMERICA

TABLE OF CONTENTS

ABOVE: Carlos Delgado, Toronto Blue Jays Top 10 Prospects For 1994. Page 64
BELOW: Kris Bryant. Chicago Cubs Top 10 Prospects For 2014. Page 40

ALL-STAR (AS) · GOLD GLOVE (GG) · MOST VALUABLE PLAYER (MVP) · CY YOUNG AWARD (CYA) · HALL OF FAME (HOF).

PLAYER	POS	SIGNED	PAGE	AWARDS & HONORS				
				AS	GG	MVP	CYA	HOF
Miguel Cabrera	1B	1999	46	11		2		
Robinson Cano	2B	2001	48	8	2			
Chris Carpenter	SP	1993	50	3			1	
Roger Clemens	SP	1983	52	11		1	7	
Gerrit Cole	SP	2011	54	2				
Bartolo Colon	SP	1993	56	4			1	
David Cone	SP	1981	58	5			1	
Johnny Cueto	SP	2004	60	2				
Jacob deGrom	SP	2010	62	2				
Carlos Delgado	1B	1988	64	2				
Eric Gagne	RP	1995	66	3			1	
Nomar Garciaparra	SS	1994	68	6				
Jason Giambi	1B	1992	70	5		1		
Tom Glavine	SP	1984	72	10			2	★
Paul Goldschmidt	1B	2009	74	6	3			
Juan Gonzalez	RF	1986	76	3		2		
Dwight Gooden	SP	1982	78	4			1	
Zack Greinke	SP	2002	80	5	4		1	
Ken Griffey Jr.	CF	1987	82	13	10	1		★
Vladimir Guerrero	RF	1993	84	9		1		★
Roy Halladay	SP	1995	86	8			2	
Cole Hamels	SP	2002	88	4				
Mike Hampton	SP	1990	90	2	1			
Bryce Harper	RF	2010	92	6		1		
Felix Hernandez	SP	2002	94	6			1	
Trevor Hoffman	RP	1989	96	7				★
Tim Hudson	SP	1997	98	4				
Derek Jeter	SS	1992	100	14	5			★
Randy Johnson	SP	1985	102	10			5	★
Andruw Jones	CF	1993	104	5	10			
Chipper Jones	3B	1990	106	8		1		★
Jeff Kent	2B	1989	108	5		1		
Clayton Kershaw	SP	2006	110	7	1	1	3	
Dallas Keuchel	SP	2009	112	2	3		1	
Craig Kimbrel	RP	2008	114	7				
Corey Kluber	SP	2007	116	3			2	
Barry Larkin	SS	1985	118	12	3	1		★
Cliff Lee	SP	2000	120	4			1	
Jon Lester	SP	2002	122	5				
Tim Lincecum	SP	2006	124	4			2	
Francisco Lindor	SS	2011	126	3	1			
Kenny Lofton	CF	1988	128	6	4			
Evan Longoria	3B	2006	130	3	3			
Manny Machado	3B	2010	132	4	2			
Greg Maddux	SP	1984	134	8	18		4	★
Russell Martin	C	2002	136	4	1			
Edgar Martinez	DH	1982	138	7				
Pedro Martinez	SP	1988	140	8			3	★
Don Mattingly	1B	1979	142	6	9	1		
Joe Mauer	C	2001	144	6	3	1		
Brian McCann	C	2002	146	7				
Andrew McCutchen	CF	2005	148	5	1	1		

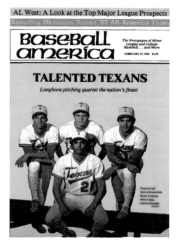

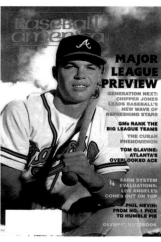

ABOVE: Roger Clemens. Boston Red Sox Top 10 Prospects For 1984. Page 52

BELOW: Chipper Jones. Atlanta Braves Top 10 Prospects For 1994. Page 106

THE 2018 GOLD GLOVE, MVP AND CY YOUNG AWARD WINNERS HAD NOT BEEN ANNOUNCED WHEN WE WENT TO PRESS.

TABLE OF CONTENTS

ALL-STAR (AS) • GOLD GLOVE (GG) • MOST VALUABLE PLAYER (MVP) • CY YOUNG AWARD (CYA) • HALL OF FAME (HOF).

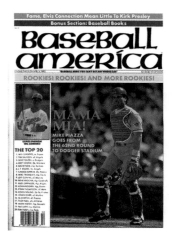

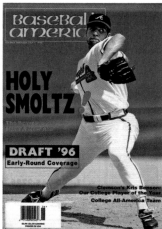

ABOVE: Mike Piazza. Los Angeles Dodgers Top 10 Prospects from 1993. Page 168

BELOW: John Smoltz. Atlanta Braves Top 10 Prospects For 1988. International League Top 10 Prospects For 1988. Page 204

ABOVE: Justin Verlander. Detroit Tigers Top 10 Prospects For 2006.
Page 232

LEFT: Frank Thomas. Chicago White Sox Top 10 Prospects For 1990. Southern League Top 10 Prospects For 1990.
Page 220

RIGHT: Larry Walker. Montreal Expos Top 10 Prospects For 1987. Montreal Expos Top 10 Prospects For 1988.
Page 242

THE 2018 GOLD GLOVE, MVP AND CY YOUNG AWARD WINNERS HAD NOT BEEN ANNOUNCED WHEN WE WENT TO PRESS.

ROBERTO ALOMAR, 2B

BIOGRAPHY

PROPER NAME: Roberto Alomar Velázquez. **BORN:** February 5, 1968 in Ponce, Puerto Rico.
HT: 6-0. **WT:** 185. **BATS:** B. **THROWS:** R. **SCHOOL:** Luis Munoz Rivera HS, Salinas, Puerto Rico.
FIRST PRO CONTRACT: Signed as international free agent by Padres, Feb. 16, 1985.

CALIFORNIA LEAGUE TOP 10 PROSPECTS FOR 1986

(Alomar) finished as the league's hitting leader at .346, and drew raves for his ability to get on base, his bunting ability and his play around second base.

It's all the more amazing because of his age — he's in his second year of pro ball at 18. His father, Sandy Alomar, spent 15 years in the majors and was a San Diego coach during the 1986 season.

"With his age and his background, he can't miss." said (Stockton Ports manager Dave) Machemer.

— **By Jim Alexander**

SAN DIEGO PADRES TOP 10 PROSPECTS FOR 1988

BACKGROUND: An exceptional second baseman, he was moved to shortstop and, despite 36 errors, made enough progress to become Garry Templeton's heir apparent. Alomar is a quick fielder, which rarely forces him to make a flat-footed throw and compensates for arm strength that is average for a shortstop.

STRENGTHS: Alomar has the offensive skills to hit first or second in the batting order. He makes contact from both sides of the plate, already has won a batting championship (.346, California League, 1986) and has extra-base power from the left side. He is a terrific bunter and is learning to utilize speed that eventually should be worth 50 stolen bases a year.

FUTURE: After Bip Roberts in 1986 and Joey Cora last season, the Padres are reluctant to push another Double-A player into the varsity lineup at second base. They plan to begin the season with him at shortstop in Las Vegas, with the idea that he will be ready to claim a middle-infield job by July.

— **By Ken Leiker**

MINOR LEAGUE MENTIONS BY BA

YEAR	TOP 100	ORG RANKING	LEAGUE RANKING	BEST TOOLS
1986		No. 4: Padres	No. 3: California	
1987		No. 4: Padres	No. 8: Texas	TL: Best Defensive SS
1988		No. 1: Padres		

BaseBall america

SECOND
TO NONE

AL DRAFT
REPORT CARDS

THE PRESSURE ON
FIRST-ROUND PICKS

BASEBALL FEVER
GRIPS SEATTLE

TONY GWYNN
AT THE MOVIES

JOSE ALTUVE, 2B

BIOGRAPHY

PROPER NAME: Jose Carlos Altuve. **BORN:** May 6, 1990 in Maracay, Venezuela.
HT: 5-6. **WT:** 165. **BATS:** R. **THROWS:** R.
FIRST PRO CONTRACT: Signed as international free agent by Astros, March 6, 2007.

HOUSTON ASTROS TOP 30 PROSPECTS FOR 2011

Altuve fits no standard profile. He doesn't lack tools, but he's difficult to compare to other players. He has a unique build, compared by some scouts to a fire hydrant, and some say he is two inches shorter than his listed height. At the end of last season, he may have been 10 pounds lighter as well. But he has baseball skills and enough tools to make things interesting.

Defense is his best attribute. He has quick, strong hands that work well at the plate and in the field. He's agile and at times a dazzling second baseman, with arm strength to turn the double play well. He has developed a good rapport with shortstop Jio Mier, whom he has played with the last two seasons, and has gotten in time at third base as well.

Offensively, Altuve shows enough power to punish mistakes but mostly plays a No. 2 hitter's game. He uses the whole field, has excellent baserunning skills that augment his average speed and shows the bat control to move runners. Altuve plays with energy that makes him a team leader and keeps winning people over.

He may put up big numbers at Lancaster this season but will have to keep proving himself at higher levels to scouts who remain skeptical of a player with such a small body.

— **By John Manuel**

MINOR LEAGUE MENTIONS BY BA

YEAR	TOP 100	ORG RANKING	LEAGUE RANKING	BEST TOOLS
2010				**SAL:** Best Defensive 2B
2011		**No. 28:** Astros	**No. 15:** California	

NOLAN ARENADO, 3B

BIOGRAPHY

PROPER NAME: Nolan James Arenado. **BORN:** April 16, 1991 in Lake Forest, Calif.
HT: 6-2. **WT:** 205. **BATS:** R. **THROWS:** R. **SCHOOL:** El Toro HS, Lake Forest, Calif.
FIRST PRO CONTRACT: Selected by Rockies in second round (59th overall) of 2009 draft;
signed July 7, 2009.

COLORADO ROCKIES TOP 10 PROSPECTS FOR 2012

After missing the first six weeks in 2010 with a groin injury, Arenado broke out in 2011, leading the minors with 122 RBIs and flourishing in the Arizona Fall League. He won AFL MVP honors after batting .388 and leading the league in hits (47), doubles (12) and extra-base hits (18). He also improved on defense, ending talk that his range and first-step quickness would prompt a move from third to first base.

Arenado has exceptional hand-eye coordination and very quick, strong hands. He entered pro ball with an advanced two-strike approach and has learned to turn on pitches when he gets the opportunity. His swing has a flat path, but he gets good extension and has shown an increased ability to hit balls with backspin, which should lead to solid or better power. He controls the strike zone well and is starting to draw more walks. Arenado dropped 20 pounds last offseason, resulting in average range at third base despite his lack of quick feet. He has soft hands and plenty of arm strength, with plus accuracy and a quick release from any angle. He's a well below-average runner.

Arenado has the work ethic to maintain his defensive skills. He's competitive but can show his youth by getting emotional at times. A potential No. 3 hitter, Arenado should open 2012 in Double-A, with a second-half promotion to the big leagues a possibility. He could be ready for a regular role in Colorado by 2013.

— By Jack Etkin

MINOR LEAGUE MENTIONS BY BA

YEAR	TOP 100	ORG RANKING	LEAGUE RANKING	BEST TOOLS
2009			**No. 8:** Pioneer	
2010		**No. 10:** Rockies	**No. 2:** South Atlantic	
2011	No. 80	**No. 3:** Rockies	**No. 6:** California	**CAL:** Best Defensive 3B
2012	No. 42	**No. 2:** Rockies	**No. 8:** Texas	**TL:** Best Defensive 3B
2013	No. 52	**No. 1:** Rockies		

JAKE ARRIETA, RHP

BIOGRAPHY

PROPER NAME: Jacob Joseph Arrieta. **BORN:** March 6, 1986 in Farmington, Mo.
HT: 6-4. **WT:** 225. **BATS:** R. **THROWS:** R. **SCHOOL:** Texas Christian.
FIRST PRO CONTRACT: Selected by Orioles in fifth round (159th overall) of 2007 draft;
signed Aug. 15, 2007.

BALTIMORE ORIOLES TOP 10 PROSPECTS FOR 2010

After leading the Carolina League in ERA and pitching in the Olympics for Team USA in 2008, Arrieta pitched his way to Triple-A in 2009 and led the organization (both major and minor leaguers) with 148 strikeouts. The Orioles signed him for a $1.1 million bonus in 2007.

Arrieta is a bulldog who is willing to challenge hitters in the strike zone. His fastball sits in the 92-94 mph range, and has the action to generate swings and misses. His slider has become a solid second pitch and is plus at times, while his changeup is solid but needs the most improvement. He also occasionally throws a curve to lefthanded hitters.

While Arrieta can throw strikes with all his pitches, he needs to do it more consistently and better command his pitches in the strike zone. His 56 walks last season were the most in the farm system. The Orioles worked to shorten his stride last season to give his pitches a better finish and keep them down. Arrieta's pure stuff compares with any of the Orioles' elite young pitchers, but his command puts him a notch behind them.

While some scouts think that could eventually send Arrieta to the bullpen, the Orioles see him as a middle-of-the-rotation pitcher who can pile up 200 innings a year with no problems.

— **By Will Lingo**

MINOR LEAGUE MENTIONS BY BA

YEAR	TOP 100	ORG RANKING	LEAGUE RANKING	BEST TOOLS
2008		**No. 7:** Orioles	**No. 2:** Carolina	**CAR:** Best Fastball
2009	No. 67	**No. 4:** Orioles	**No. 17:** Eastern **No. 11:** International	
2010	No. 99	**No. 4:** Orioles	**No. 14:** International	

JEFF BAGWELL, 1B

BIOGRAPHY

PROPER NAME: Jeffrey Robert Bagwell. **BORN:** May 27, 1968 in Boston, Mass.
HT: 6-0. **WT:** 195. **BATS:** R. **THROWS:** R. **SCHOOL:** Hartford.
FIRST PRO CONTRACT: Selected by Red Sox in fourth round (110th overall) of 1989 draft;
signed June 10, 1989.

EASTERN LEAGUE TOP 10 PROSPECTS FOR 1990

Bagwell's numbers were staggering in his first professional season. He finished second in hitting, playing half his games at Beehive Field, one of the toughest parks for hitters in the minors. Bagwell broke the New Britain season record for hits, led the league in hits and doubles and was second in triples.

Said Canton manager Ken Bolek: "He's proved day in, day out that he's the best hitter in the league. And the amazing thing is that he's been steady all year. This is his first full year, and he's proved himself in a very difficult league."

In a move to shore up their bullpen, the Red Sox traded Bagwell to the Astros for reliever Larry Andersen.

— **By Phil Bowman**

HOUSTON ASTROS TOP 10 PROSPECTS FOR 1991

Boston's decision to trade Bagwell to Houston after the minor league season was not a popular one in New England. Bagwell was a University of Hartford product, one of New England's own.

Bagwell missed winning the Eastern League batting title by one point in 1990, a significant feat for a below-average runner. He's got an excellent stroke, takes pitches well, makes contact and uses the whole park.

Bagwell is not Ken Caminiti at third base, though he has a chance to inherit his job this spring if Caminiti is dealt for much-needed pitching. He does not have Caminiti's superb arm, but is considered an above-average thrower.

— **By Allan Simpson**

MINOR LEAGUE MENTIONS BY BA

YEAR	TOP 100	ORG RANKING	LEAGUE RANKING	BEST TOOLS
1990			**No. 4:** Eastern	**EL:** Best Hitter
1991	No. 32	**No. 2:** Astros		

JOSH BECKETT, RHP

BIOGRAPHY

PROPER NAME: Josh Patrick Beckett. **BORN:** May 15, 1980 in Spring, Texas.
HT: 6-5. **WT:** 230. **BATS:** R. **THROWS:** R. **SCHOOL:** Spring (Texas) HS.
FIRST PRO CONTRACT: Selected by Marlins in first round (second overall) of 1999 draft;
signed Sept. 1, 1999.

FLORIDA MARLINS TOP 10 PROSPECTS FOR 2000

BACKGROUND: Beckett was drafted No. 2 overall in June, becoming the first high school righthander since Bill Gullickson (1979) to be taken that high. He signed a four-year, $7 million major league contract just days before he was to head to Blinn (Texas) Junior College.

STRENGTHS: Beckett is the same age as many college sophomores. He has a prototypical power pitcher's build and has been clocked as high as 97 mph, though he topped out at 94 during instructional league. He has a devastating 12-to-6 curveball that breaks hard and late. Though extremely confident, Beckett is coachable and willing to learn.

WEAKNESSES: Beckett is inexperienced and needs to work on finishing his pitches. His changeup is still developing, but the arm speed and command are there already.

FUTURE: He will begin 2000 at either low Class A Kane County or at high Class A Brevard County. All indications point to a rapid pass through the Marlins' system.

— **By Mike Berardino**

MINOR LEAGUE MENTIONS BY BA

YEAR	TOP 100	ORG RANKING	LEAGUE RANKING	BEST TOOLS
2000	No. 19	**No. 2:** Marlins	**No. 1:** Midwest	**MWL:** Best Fastball
2001	No. 3	**No. 1:** Marlins	**No. 1:** Florida State **No. 1:** Eastern	**FSL:** Best Pitching Prospect, Best Fastball, Best Breaking Pitch **EL:** Best Pitching Prospect
2002	No. 1	**No. 1:** Marlins		

ALBERT BELLE, OF

BIOGRAPHY

PROPER NAME: Albert Jojuan Belle. **BORN:** August 25, 1966 in Shreveport, La.
HT: 6-2. **WT:** 210. **BATS:** R. **THROWS:** R. **SCHOOL:** Louisiana State.
FIRST PRO CONTRACT: Selected by Indians in second round (47th overall) of 1987 draft;
signed Aug. 27, 1987.

TOP COLLEGE PROSPECTS FOR 1987 DRAFT

Of eight college outfielders drawing interest from national crosscheckers, Louisiana State's Joey Belle is the only one who rates the consensus of scouts as a No. 1 pick.

"He doesn't always give the impression he wants to play," said one scouting director, "but on tools alone he's a first-rounder. He's got power, he can run, and he has a right fielder's arm."

— **By Allan Simpson**

CLEVELAND INDIANS TOP 10 PROSPECTS FOR 1988

A second-round pick out of Louisiana State (the Indians lost their No. 1 selection for signing Rick Dempsey, of all people), Belle has the best pure talent in the organization. In fact, many scouts say based on talent he might have been the best player available in last June's draft.

The problem is, attitude is a big part of this game, and Belle has to learn to control his emotions if he's ever going to make the most of his ability. Things got so out of hand at LSU last year that he was thrown off the team and didn't even go to the College World Series.

There also was a flareup in the Florida Instructional League, but Belle was back, after apologizing for his actions, the next day. He can run, throw and hit for average as well as power.

— **By Tracy Ringolsby**

MINOR LEAGUE MENTIONS BY BA

YEAR	TOP 100	ORG RANKING	LEAGUE RANKING	BEST TOOLS
1988		No. 6: Indians		
1989		No. 3: Indians	No. 1: Eastern	EL: Best Hitter, Best Power

CARLOS BELTRAN, OF

BIOGRAPHY

PROPER NAME: Carlos Ivan Beltran. **BORN:** April 24, 1977 in Manati, Puerto Rico.
HT: 6-1. **WT:** 215. **BATS:** B. **THROWS:** R. **SCHOOL:** Fernando Callejo HS, Manati, Puerto Rico.
FIRST PRO CONTRACT: Selected by Royals in second round (49th overall) of the 1995 draft;
signed June 5, 1995.

KANSAS CITY ROYALS TOP 10 PROSPECTS FOR 1998

BACKGROUND: Beltran skipped low Class A in 1997 but struggled offensively in the high Class A Carolina League. He rebounded with a strong winter in his native Puerto Rico (.241-3-20 in 162 at-bats for Arecibo) and played in that league's all-star game.

STRENGTHS: A quality athlete with easy actions, Beltran has the chance to be a five-tool player with increased strength and hitting skills. He is already the organization's best defensive center fielder and is developing more power in his swing.

WEAKNESSES: Beltran's progress will be dictated by his bat, which has plenty of holes. For one of the fastest players in the organization, he is not an accomplished baserunner and basestealer.

FUTURE: Beltran's success this winter in Puerto Rico will give him a shot at Double-A in 1998 if he has a strong spring showing.

— **By David Rawnsley**

MINOR LEAGUE MENTIONS BY BA

YEAR	TOP 100	ORG RANKING	LEAGUE RANKING	BEST TOOLS
1995			**No. 9:** Gulf Coast	
1996		**No. 4:** Royals	**No. 8:** Northwest	
1997	No. 93	**No. 2:** Royals		**CAR:** Best Defensive OF
1998		**No. 5:** Royals	**No. 7:** Carolina **No. 5:** Texas	**CAR:** Best Defensive OF, Best OF Arm, Most Exciting Player
1999	No. 14	**No 1:** Royals		

ADRIAN BELTRE, 3B

BIOGRAPHY

PROPER NAME: Adrian Beltre Perez.
BORN: April 7, 1979 in Santo Domingo, Dominican Republic.
HT: 5-11. **WT:** 220. **BATS:** R. **THROWS:** R. **SCHOOL:** Liceo Maximo Gomez, Santo Domingo, Dominican Republic.
FIRST PRO CONTRACT: Signed as international free agent by Dodgers, July 7, 1994.

LOS ANGELES DODGERS TOP 10 PROSPECTS FOR 1998

BACKGROUND: Beltre was the Florida State League's top prospect after contending for a triple crown. The Dodgers, who have often rushed their position prospects, have shown unusual patience with Beltre, letting him spend two full years in Class A.

STRENGTHS: Beltre may be the most gifted player in the minors. All his tools are at least above-average. His hitting and power are on par with (Paul) Konerko's. He has above-average speed and the strongest arm in the organization outside of Raul Mondesi.

WEAKNESSES: Any weakness in Beltre's package would be a matter of comparison to his own tools. He hasn't shown any weaknesses in two years of minor league ball.

FUTURE: Beltre would be considered the top prospect in just about any organization. The most likely scenario is for Beltre to take over third in 1999, with Konerko at first.

— **By David Rawnsley**

MINOR LEAGUE MENTIONS BY BA

YEAR	TOP 100	ORG RANKING	LEAGUE RANKING	BEST TOOLS
1996			**No. 1:** South Atlantic **No. 9:** California	**SAL:** Best Hitter, Best Power, Best Defensive 3B, Best INF Arm, Most Exciting Player
1997	No. 30	**No. 4:** Dodgers	**No. 1:** Florida State	**FSL:** Best Hitter, Best Power, Best Defensive 3B, Best INF Arm, Most Exciting Player
1998	No. 3	**No. 2:** Dodgers	**No. 1:** Texas	**TL:** Best Hitter, Best Defensive 3B, Best INF Arm, Most Exciting Player

MOOKIE BETTS, OF

BIOGRAPHY

PROPER NAME: Markus Lynn Betts. **BORN:** October 7, 1992 in Brentwood, Tenn.
HT: 5-9. **WT:** 180. **BATS:** R. **THROWS:** R. **SCHOOL:** Overton HS, Brentwood, Tenn.
FIRST PRO CONTRACT: Selected by Red Sox in fifth round (172nd overall) of 2011 draft;
signed June 7, 2011.

BOSTON RED SOX TOP 10 PROSPECTS FOR 2014

No one more significantly redefined his prospect status in the system in 2013 quite like Betts. Drafted as a multi-sport athlete (baseball, basketball, bowling), he showed a line-drive swing, good strike-zone judgment, speed and no power (zero homers) at short-season Lowell in 2012. That changed in 2013, when he showed improved patience and drove the ball for extra bases with startling frequency, first at low Class A Greenville then at high Class A Salem.

Betts joined eight other minor leaguers with at least 15 homers and 30 steals in 2013. Though he has a sizable leg kick, Betts has the body control and athleticism to maintain balance, the quick hands to let the ball travel and the hand-eye coordination and bat speed to produce extra-base power. He shows a penchant for highlight-reel defensive plays at second base, and he has the athleticism and range for the Red Sox to consider shortstop and center field as possibilities. Betts' arm is better suited for the right side of the infield. He pairs above-average speed with good reads to steal bases at an excellent rate.

With Dustin Pedroia signed for eight years, Betts' future with organization, barring a trade, is most likely at any position but the one he's playing. He appears headed for Double-A Portland in 2014.

— **By Alex Speier**

MINOR LEAGUE MENTIONS BY BA

YEAR	TOP 100	ORG RANKING	LEAGUE RANKING	BEST TOOLS
2013		**No. 31:** Red Sox	**No. 8:** South Atlantic **No. 7:** Carolina	**SAL:** Best Strike-Zone Judgment
2014	No. 75	**No. 7:** Red Sox	**No. 2:** Eastern **No. 2:** International	**EL:** Best Defensive 2B

CRAIG BIGGIO, 2B

BIOGRAPHY

PROPER NAME: Craig Alan Biggio. **BORN:** December 14, 1965 in Smithtown, N.Y.
HT: 5-11. **WT:** 185. **BATS:** R. **THROWS:** R. **SCHOOL:** Seton Hall.
FIRST PRO CONTRACT: Selected by Astros in first round (22nd overall) of 1987 draft;
signed June 8, 1987.

SOUTH ATLANTIC LEAGUE TOP 10 PROSPECTS FOR 1987

Managers were in agreement that Biggio, Houston's No. 1 draft pick in June, has all the tools and all the right intangibles to make the major leagues.

The disagreement is where. Few think it will be as a catcher.

"He is definitely the top prospect or among the top two," (manager Keith) Bodie said. "He probably will play in the big leagues before anyone in this league."

Why? Biggio can hit, hit with power, throw and run. He stole 31 bases, while batting .375, in just 64 games. The opinions on his arm strength varied from good to fair. Managers also raved about his desire (and) hustle.

— By Richard Chesley

HOUSTON ASTROS TOP 10 PROSPECTS FOR 1988

The Astros' No. 1 selection last June out of Seton Hall, Biggio has the tools to develop into a solid big league player.

He has power (17 doubles, nine home runs and 49 RBIs in 216 at-bats at Class A Asheville in his taste at pro ball). He has speed (31 stolen bases). And he knows the strike zone (39 walks and 33 strikeouts).

The question, though, is where Biggio will eventually play in the big leagues. For now, the Astros will try to refine him into a decent catcher. He is part of that new breed of one-handed catchers who is going to have to make marked improvement in the quickness with which he moves his free hand. His throwing mechanics also need refining.

— By Tracy Ringolsby

MINOR LEAGUE MENTIONS BY BA

YEAR	TOP 100	ORG RANKING	LEAGUE RANKING	BEST TOOLS
1987			No. 4: South Atlantic	
1988		No. 1: Astros		

BARRY BONDS, OF

BIOGRAPHY

PROPER NAME: Barry Lamar Bonds. **BORN:** July 24, 1964 in Riverside, Calif.
HT: 6-2. **WT:** 240. **BATS:** L. **THROWS:** L. **SCHOOL:** Arizona State.
FIRST PRO CONTRACT: Selected by Pirates in first round (sixth overall) of 1985 draft;
signed June 5, 1985.

TOP COLLEGE PROSPECTS FOR 1985 DRAFT

In terms of raw potential, (Bonds) may have more to offer than any player in the country, but scouts question his makeup and the way he has progressed in three seasons at Arizona State.

The son of former major league star Bobby Bonds, he can run and hit with the same kind of power his father once did. (He) hit .360 with 11 homers, 55 RBIs and 30 stolen bases in 1984 for the Sun Devils, but has missed several games this season with a knee injury.

— By Allan Simpson

PITTSBURGH PIRATES TOP 10 PROSPECTS FOR 1986

The sixth player chosen in last June's draft, there's no question about his talent. On skills alone, he probably would have been the first player taken, but some teams were scared off by what one scout described as "a Mel Hall mentality — talk, talk, talk, me, me, me." The Pirates prefer to call it "a healthy confidence."

Bonds had no trouble adjusting to a wooden bat at Prince William (.299, 13 HR, 37 RBIs, 15 SB), and he also showed more consistent power than he had at Arizona State. His announced goal of following in the footsteps of his father Bobby, as a 30-30 (homers, stolen bases) player in the big leagues may not be out of the question, although he's more of a runner than a base stealer.

He's instinctive in center field and can cover the alleys, but his arm may keep him in left. The early reports on his play in Venezuela this winter were so good the Pirates were beginning to have ideas about him possibly jumping to the varsity in the spring.

— By Ken Leiker

MINOR LEAGUE MENTIONS BY BA

YEAR	TOP 100	ORG RANKING	LEAGUE RANKING	BEST TOOLS
1986		No. 1: Pirates		

RYAN BRAUN, OF

BIOGRAPHY

PROPER NAME: Ryan Joseph Braun. **BORN:** November 17, 1983 in Mission Hills, Calif.
HT: 6-2. **WT:** 205. **BATS:** R. **THROWS:** R. **SCHOOL:** Miami.
FIRST PRO CONTRACT: Selected by Brewers in first round (fifth overall) of 2005 draft;
signed June 18, 2005.

MILWAUKEE BREWERS TOP 10 PROSPECTS FOR 2007

BACKGROUND: Like Yovani Gallardo, Braun earned a trip to the Futures Game and a promotion to Double-A, where he stepped up his performance in the second half. The fifth overall pick in the 2005 draft, he rated as the top position prospect in the Florida State League.

STRENGTHS: A rare five-tool corner infielder, Braun has tremendous bat speed and profiles as an impact hitter for average and power. He stays back on offspeed pitches and uses the entire field. His speed and arm strength are plus tools as well. He took yoga classes with Mike Lieberthal last offseason to improve his balance.

WEAKNESSES: After making 31 errors last season, Braun must improve his footwork at third base. Some scouts believe he'll eventually need to move to the outfield, but Milwaukee believes he'll be a sound defender at the hot corner. He doesn't have the most textbook swing, but it works for him.

BACKGROUND: After hitting .326 in the Arizona Fall League, Braun definitely is ready for Triple-A. The Brewers expect him to complete their home-grown infield by 2008, though he could arrive by the all-star break.

— **By Tom Haudricourt**

MINOR LEAGUE MENTIONS BY BA

YEAR	TOP 100	ORG RANKING	LEAGUE RANKING	BEST TOOLS
2005			**No. 5:** South Atlantic	
2006	No. 49	**No. 3:** Brewers	**No. 4:** Florida State **No. 6:** Southern	**FSL:** Best Hitter, Best Defensive 3B
2007	No. 26	**No. 2:** Brewers		**PCL:** Best Hitter, Most Exciting Player

KEVIN BROWN, RHP

BIOGRAPHY

PROPER NAME: James Kevin Brown. **BORN:** March 14, 1965 in Milledgeville, Ga.
HT: 6-4. **WT:** 195. **BATS:** R. **THROWS:** R. **SCHOOL:** Georgia Tech.
FIRST PRO CONTRACT: Selected by Rangers in first round (fourth overall) of 1986 draft;
singed July 17, 1986.

TOP COLLEGE PROSPECTS FOR 1986 DRAFT

For a player who went undrafted out of high school and had to be coaxed by Georgia Tech coaches to walk on as a freshman, Brown's come a long way. He's no longer the skinny righthander with the fastball in the low 80s; now he's filled out to a more ideal pitcher's build of 6-3, 175, and he's developed into a power pitcher, throwing in the upper 80s. Some scouts have him ranked right behind (Texas lefthander Greg) Swindell in sizing up this year's pitching crop.

— By Allan Simpson

TEXAS RANGERS TOP 10 PROSPECTS FOR 1989

The Rangers' No. 1 draft pick out of Georgia Tech in 1986 turned looming disaster into the system's best hope during the 1988 season. After winning on Opening Day, 1987, Brown went on a 14-game losing streak, which included his first three decisions of 1988. By early June, he was 2-7 with Tulsa and on the verge of demotion to Class A for the second year in a row.

Bang. Brown found that 95 mph fastball, combined it with his version of a split-finger pitch, and he suddenly matured. He didn't let what he felt was a bad play or a bad call rattle him. And Brown finished up the 1988 season by winning 10 of his final 12 decisions at Tulsa, with a sub-2.00 ERA.

He could be rushed into the big leagues right now, but with the winter addition of Nolan Ryan, the Rangers won't have to do that. Brown will probably go to Triple-A, where he can refine a changeup that he didn't throw in college because his fastball so overpowered hitters.

— By Tracy Ringolsby

MINOR LEAGUE MENTIONS BY BA

YEAR	TOP 100	ORG RANKING	LEAGUE RANKING	BEST TOOLS
1987		**No. 1:** Rangers		
1988		**No. 4:** Rangers	**No. 6:** Texas	
1989		**No. 1:** Rangers		

KRIS BRYANT, 3B

BIOGRAPHY

PROPER NAME: Kristopher Lee Bryant. **BORN:** January 4, 1992 in Las Vegas.
HT: 6-5. **WT:** 230. **BATS:** R. **THROWS:** R. **SCHOOL:** San Diego.
FIRST PRO CONTRACT: Selected by Cubs in first round (second overall) of 2013 draft;
signed July 12, 2013.

CHICAGO CUBS TOP 10 PROSPECTS FOR 2014

Bryant was an 18th-round pick out of Las Vegas' Bonanza High in 2010 but attended San Diego instead. After hitting 23 home runs in his first two seasons, Bryant was BA's College Player of the Year as a junior, leading the nation in home runs (31), walks, total bases and slugging. The Cubs drafted him No. 2 overall, and he got the largest signing bonus in franchise history and in the 2013 draft, at $6,708,400. He hit nine homers in his debut and helped high Class A Daytona win the Florida State League title.

Tall, lean and athletic, Bryant has all-star tools. He adjusted as a junior by spreading out in the batter's box, lowering his head and eliminating pre-swing movement. He can still get a bit uphill with his swing but now punishes the low ball. He has the leverage and loft in his swing to produce 40 homers annually while being an above-average hitter.

Bryant's easy arm strength fits well at third base, and he has solid infield actions, but he's tall for the position and some scouts consider him a better fit for right field. He played some right and even center field in college thanks to his average speed and long strides.

Bryant's torrid Arizona Fall League tour indicates he is on the fast track to Wrigley Field. If he moves quickly, he likely will shift to an outfield corner.

— By John Manuel

MINOR LEAGUE MENTIONS BY BA

YEAR	TOP 100	ORG RANKING	LEAGUE RANKING	BEST TOOLS
2013			**No. 1:** Northwest	
2014	No. 8	**No. 2:** Cubs	**No. 1:** Southern **No. 1:** Pacific Coast	**SL:** Best Hitter, Best Power, Best INF Arm **PCL:** Best Defensive 3B
2015	No. 1	**No. 1:** Cubs		

BaseBall america

MAJOR • MINORS • PROSPECTS • DRAFT • COLLEGE • HIGH SCHOOL

PLUS

Complete End Of Season
Statistics For Every
Minor League Team

We Pick Top Farm
System Performers For
Every Organization

Three Red Sox Prospects
Land On Our Minor
League All-Star Team

All-Stars At Every
Classification

Jesus Montero's
Descent Takes
A Bizarre Turn

SMASH HIT

CUBS SLUGGER KRIS BRYANT IS OUR
MINOR LEAGUE PLAYER OF THE YEAR

MARK BUEHRLE, LHP

BIOGRAPHY

PROPER NAME: Mark Alan Buehrle. **BORN:** March 23, 1979 in St. Charles, Mo.
HT: 6-2. **WT:** 240. **BATS:** L. **THROWS:** L. **SCHOOL:** Jefferson (Mo.) JC.
FIRST PRO CONTRACT: Selected by White Sox in 38th round (1,139th overall) of 1998 draft; signed May 21, 1999.

CHICAGO WHITE SOX TOP 10 PROSPECTS FOR 2000

BACKGROUND: As a 1998 draft-and-follow, Buehrle improved enough to not only sign for a low six-figure bonus, but also get sent straight to Burlington, where he acquitted himself while pitching the Bees to a Midwest League title.

STRENGTHS: Buehrle has a complete assortment of pitches that he can throw for strikes, including an 88-90 mph fastball, two types of sliders, a curveball and changeup. The command of his breaking pitches is advanced for his age, and he consistently overmatched lefthanded hitters in the Midwest League.

WEAKNESSES: The White Sox are hard-pressed to identify a weakness in Buehrle. His fringe-average fastball may be his weakest pitch.

FUTURE: Buehrle could become the fastest moving pitcher in the White Sox system. The organization has few lefthanded relievers, and though his five-pitch arsenal profiles him as a starter, short-term needs may put him in the bullpen almost immediately.

— By David Rawnsley

SOUTHERN LEAGUE TOP 10 PROSPECTS FOR 2000

Buehrle has gone from anonymity to the majors in about a year. He gave up five earned runs in his first outing for Birmingham, then never gave up more than three in his next 15 starts, earning a promotion to Chicago.

"Buehrle is special because he's a four-pitch pitcher who can find the strike zone with all four pitches," Birmingham manager Nick Capra said.

He has no apparent weakness. Buehrle has an average fastball, terrific command of his curveball and slider, and a nifty changeup.

— By David Jenkins

MINOR LEAGUE MENTIONS BY BA

YEAR	TOP 100	ORG RANKING	LEAGUE RANKING	BEST TOOLS
2000		**No. 10:** White Sox	**No. 9:** Southern	**SL:** Best Control

MADISON BUMGARNER, LHP

BIOGRAPHY

PROPER NAME: Madison Kyle Bumgarner. **BORN:** August 1, 1989 in Hickory, N.C.
HT: 6-4. **WT:** 242. **BATS:** R. **THROWS:** L. **SCHOOL:** South Caldwell HS, Hudson, N.C.
FIRST PRO CONTRACT: Selected by Giants in first round (10th overall) of 2007 draft;
signed Aug. 14, 2007.

SAN FRANCISCO GIANTS TOP 10 PROSPECTS FOR 2010

Bumgarner ranked third in the minors with a 1.85 ERA last season after leading the minors with a 1.46 mark in 2008. Nevertheless, his heady stock dipped slightly as his velocity waned. The 10th overall pick in 2007, he signed for $2 million.

At his best, Bumgarner shows a mid-90s fastball, a slider with good tilt and an average changeup. His heater has late giddy-up and he has advanced command of it. His easy, three-quarters delivery adds deception. He works the ladder, loves to throw upstairs and gets the ball inside against lefties and righties alike. He's an ornery competitor in the mold of Kevin Brown, and when the Giants needed him to make his major league debut on an hour's notice, he showed zero fear. He's a good athlete who helps himself with the bat.

Bumgarner pitched at 88-90 mph for most of the second half of last season. A perfectionist, he may have lost velocity because he threw too much on the side. His slider still isn't a finished product and his changeup isn't entirely trustworthy. He defaults to his fastball when he gets in jams. He must learn to control his emotions and trust his catcher.

Bumgarner has No. 1 starter potential, and his stuff would play against big leaguers now. He's just 20, so they'd prefer to let him work in Triple-A to start 2010.

— **By Andy Baggarly**

MINOR LEAGUE MENTIONS BY BA

YEAR	TOP 100	ORG RANKING	LEAGUE RANKING	BEST TOOLS
2008		**No. 3:** Giants	**No. 1:** South Atlantic	**SAL:** Best Pitching Prospect, Best Control
2009	No. 9	**No. 1:** Giants	**No. 2:** Eastern	**CAL:** Best Pitching Prospect
2010	No. 14	**No. 2:** Giants	**No. 4:** Pacific Coast	**PCL:** Best Pitching Prospect

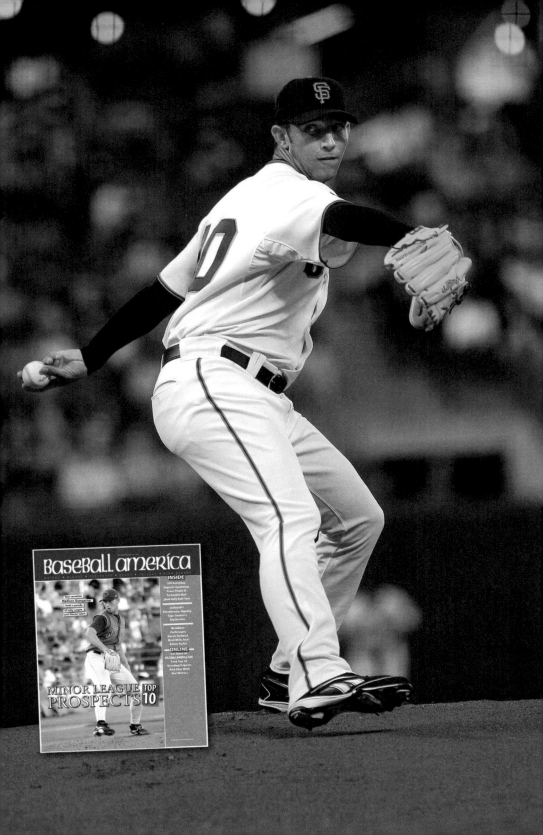

MIGUEL CABRERA, 1B

BIOGRAPHY

PROPER NAME: Jose Miguel Cabrera. **BORN:** April 18, 1993 in Maracay, Venezuela.
HT: 6-4. **WT:** 249. **BATS:** R. **THROWS:** R. **SCHOOL:** Maracay, Venezuela.
FIRST PRO CONTRACT: Signed as international free agent by Marlins, July 2, 1999.

FLORIDA MARLINS TOP 10 PROSPECTS FOR 2002

Signed for a Venezuelan-record $1.9 million, Cabrera grew up with a diamond just beyond his back yard, and his instincts show as much. Last July in Seattle, he became the youngest player in the short history of the Futures Game.

Cabrera plays with an all-around smoothness that makes him stand out, even on a Class A Kane County club that also included Adrian Gonzalez. Cabrera does everything with apparent ease, including driving the ball with authority into both gaps and producing runs in RBI situations. He has a good idea of the strike zone for such a young player. He has plus range and arm strength.

Cabrera shed baby fat and became much lighter on his feet with a well-defined physique. Despite the increased quickness, Cabrera's speed is below-average due to his thick legs. He hasn't shown much home run power, but that should come.

He missed time in 2001 with a lower back problem, the only thing that could slow what figures to be a rapid rise. Cabrera could make the jump to Double-A to start 2002, and he'll continue to play shortstop primarily. An eventual move to third base no longer is considered essential.

— By Mike Berardino

MINOR LEAGUE MENTIONS BY BA

YEAR	TOP 100	ORG RANKING	LEAGUE RANKING	BEST TOOLS
2000		**No. 11:** Marlins		
2001	No. 91	**No. 3:** Marlins	**No. 9:** Midwest	**MWL:** Best INF Arm
2002	No. 38	**No. 2:** Marlins	**No. 5:** Florida State	
2003	No. 12	**No. 1:** Marlins	**No. 1:** Southern	**SL:** Best Hitter, Best Strike-Zone Judgment, Best Defensive 3B, Best INF Arm, Most Exciting Player

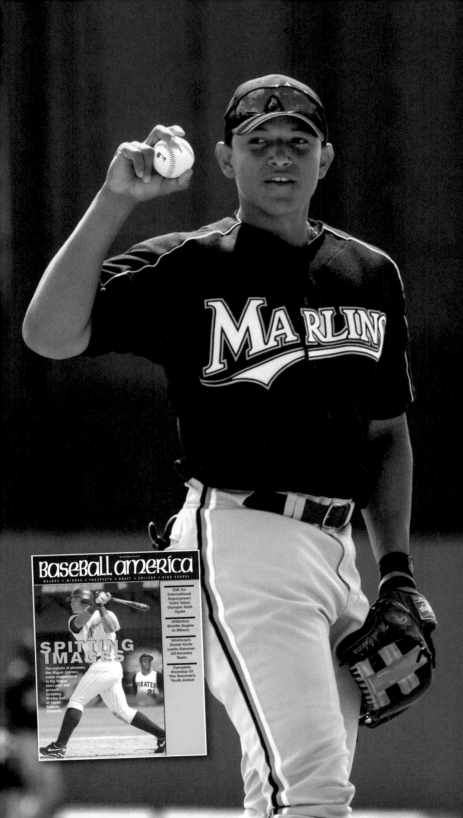

ROBINSON CANO, 2B

BIOGRAPHY

PROPER NAME: Robinson Jose Cano.
BORN: October 22, 1982 in San Pedro de Macoris, Dominican Republic.
HT: 6-0. **WT:** 210. **BATS:** L. **THROWS:** R. **SCHOOL:** San Pedro de Macoris, Dominican Republic.
FIRST PRO CONTRACT: Signed as international free agent by Yankees, Jan. 5, 2001.

NEW YORK YANKEES TOP 10 PROSPECTS FOR 2005

Cano's name was tossed around in trade rumors when the Yankees unsuccessfully tried to acquire Randy Johnson at the July 31 deadline, but he was not part of the deal when New York finally got Johnson over the winter. A confident player, Cano plays as if he belongs in the majors. His father Jose pitched briefly in the big leagues.

Cano's arm is his best tool and rates as a 65 on the 20-80 scouting scale. More important, he can hit. He has good bat speed and a fluid swing, allowing him to catch up to good fastballs. His improving plate discipline helped his power numbers increase; he set career highs in walks and slugging in 2004.

Cano hasn't handled lefthanders well, with just seven extra base hits in 130 at-bats against southpaws above Class A. He's a below-average runner for an infielder, and his lower half figures to get thicker as he gets older. He has solid infield actions and the Yankees refute reports that he has below-average range.

Cano could be a bench option in New York for 2005, but he'll likely head back to Columbus for a full season in Triple-A after the Yankees signed free agent Tony Womack.

— **By John Manuel**

MINOR LEAGUE MENTIONS BY BA

YEAR	TOP 100	ORG RANKING	LEAGUE RANKING	BEST TOOLS
2002			**No. 11:** New York-Penn	
2003		**No. 8:** Yankees	**No. 18:** Florida State	**FSL:** Best Defensive 2B
2004		**No. 6:** Yankees	**No. 16:** Eastern **No. 14:** International	**EL:** Best Defensive 2B
2005		**No. 2:** Yankees		

CHRIS CARPENTER, RHP

BIOGRAPHY

PROPER NAME: Christopher John Carpenter. **BORN:** April 27, 1975 in Exeter, N.H.
HT: 6-6. **WT:** 230. **BATS:** R. **THROWS:** R. **SCHOOL:** Trinity HS, Manchester, N.H.
FIRST PRO CONTRACT: Selected by Blue Jays in first round (15th overall) of 1993 draft;
signed Aug. 10, 1993.

TORONTO BLUE JAYS TOP 10 PROSPECTS FOR 1995

BACKGROUND: After missing his first summer in a prolonged negotiation, Carpenter has been slowed by physical problems in the past two instructional leagues. First it was a back problem in 1993, and most recently tenderness in his right arm.

STRENGTHS: With his size and arm strength, Carpenter reminds some of Curt Schilling. But he's bigger than Schilling, and has a better mental makeup. With a mid-90s fastball and a power curve, Carpenter will advance quickly if he stays healthy.

WEAKNESSES: Like many young pitchers, Carpenter dominates at the lower levels with his hard stuff. He will have to develop an advanced offspeed pitch to go with his fastball. Other than that, all he needs is experience.

FUTURE: None of the physical problems that has slowed Carpenter is considered serious. He won't turn 20 until after the 1995 season begins, so there's no sense in rushing him. The South Atlantic League would be a good place to start the year.

— **By Tracy Ringolsby**

MINOR LEAGUE MENTIONS BY BA

YEAR	TOP 100	ORG RANKING	LEAGUE RANKING	BEST TOOLS
1994			No. 3: Pioneer	
1995	No. 100	No. 5: Blue Jays		
1996	No. 82	No. 3: Blue Jays		
1997	No. 28	No. 3: Blue Jays	No. 10: International	

ROGER CLEMENS, RHP

BIOGRAPHY

PROPER NAME: William Roger Clemens. **BORN:** August 4, 1962 in Dayton, Ohio.
HT: 6-4. **WT:** 235. **BATS:** R. **THROWS:** R. **SCHOOL:** Texas.
FIRST PRO CONTRACT: Selected by Red Sox in first round (19th overall) of 1983 draft;
signed June 21, 1983.

BOSTON RED SOX TOP 10 PROSPECTS FOR 1984

The most accomplished pitcher from last June's draft, Clemens is expected to start the season in Triple-A, but some scouts say he is ready for the varsity rotation. If Dennis Eckersley is traded, part of the reason likely will be because the Red Sox think Clemens can fill the spot in the rotation.

In 11 pro starts last season after helping the University of Texas win the NCAA championship, Clemens had a 7-2 record, 1.33 ERA, 95 strikeouts and only 12 walks in 81 innings. He was equally dominant in both the Florida State League and the Eastern League.

Clemens' fastball approaches 90 mph, he has two speeds on his curveball, and he is developing a forkball that will serve as a changeup. Scouts say that his delivery is flawless—each pitch coming from the same motion—and that he puts the ball on a hitter's wrists as well as any young pitcher in years.

— By Ken Leiker

FLORIDA STATE LEAGUE TOP 10 PROSPECTS FOR 1983

After he lost a close 1-0 game to Vero Beach in July, veteran Dodgers manager Stan Wasiak was talking not so much about his team's win as he was the control of Clemens.

"Whatever they spent on him," Wasiak exclaimed, "it was worth it. He has to be one of the best pitching prospects I've seen this year."

Although he appeared in only four games at Winter Haven before being called up to New Britain (Eastern), Clemens was named by virtually everyone in the league responding to the Baseball America survey. He was also named the top prospect in the Eastern League.

— By Joe Sanchez

MINOR LEAGUE MENTIONS BY BA

YEAR	TOP 100	ORG RANKING	LEAGUE RANKING	BEST TOOLS
1984		**No. 1:** Red Sox	**No. 3:** Florida State **No. 1:** Eastern	

GERRIT COLE, RHP

BIOGRAPHY

PROPER NAME: Gerrit Alan Cole. **BORN:** September 8, 1990 in Newport Beach, Calif.
HT: 6-4. **WT:** 225. **BATS:** R. **THROWS:** R. **SCHOOL:** UCLA.
FIRST PRO CONTRACT: Selected by Pirates in first round (first overall) of 2011 draft;
signed Aug. 15, 2011.

PITTSBURGH PIRATES TOP 10 PROSPECTS FOR 2012

The Pirates made Cole the No. 1 overall choice in the 2011 draft and gave him a draft-record $8 million bonus at the Aug. 15 signing deadline.

Cole signed too late to play in the minors but did participate in the Arizona Fall League, where he lit up radar guns with a fastball that reached as high as 102 mph. He usually worked at 93-98 mph at UCLA, with better command when he stayed at the low end of that range. As he gains experience, he could throw harder while doing a better job of locating his fastball. Cole also has a wipeout slider that drops off the table just as it reaches home plate. It's a true swing-and-miss pitch that earns plus-plus grades at times. So too does his changeup, though it's less reliable than his slider.

Cole's biggest challenge is to become more consistent with his delivery. Though he has enviable mechanics when he is right, he has spells where he begins flying open with his front shoulder and loses command of his pitches. He also has a tendency to drive too much off his back leg, which causes his front foot to land hard and also affects his ability to put his pitches where he wants. Cole has the athleticism that will allow him to repeat his delivery and the size and strength to be a workhorse at the top of a rotation.

Cole is advanced enough to make his pro debut at Double-A Altoona. He could push his way to Triple-A Indianapolis before the end of 2012 and shouldn't need much more than a year in the minors before he can help Pittsburgh. He's one of the few pitching prospects with legitimate ace potential.

— **By John Perrotto**

MINOR LEAGUE MENTIONS BY BA

YEAR	TOP 100	ORG RANKING	LEAGUE RANKING	BEST TOOLS
2012	No. 12	**No. 1:** Pirates	**No. 2:** Florida State **No. 3:** Eastern	**FSL:** Best Fastball
2013	No. 7	**No. 1:** Pirates	**No. 3:** International	**IL:** Best Pitching Prospect

BARTOLO COLON, RHP

BIOGRAPHY

PROPER NAME: Bartolo Colon. **BORN:** May 24, 1973 in Altamira, Dominican Republic.
HT: 5-11. **WT:** 285. **BATS:** R. **THROWS:** R. **SCHOOL:** Puerto Plata, Dominican Republic.
FIRST PRO CONTRACT: Signed as international free agent by Indians, June 26, 1993.

CLEVELAND INDIANS TOP 10 PROSPECTS FOR 1996

BACKGROUND: Despite not pitching after Aug. 1 because of a bone bruise in his elbow, Colon was so dominant at Kinston that he was named the Carolina League pitcher of the year and the league's top prospect. He's a comet hurtling toward the big leagues. He has gone 26-8, 2.52 while giving up an average of just 6.2 hits per nine innings in his three professional seasons.

STRENGTHS: When opposing teams discuss trades with Hart, Colon's name is always one of the first mentioned. He's the premier pitcher in a pitching-rich system. He has three quality pitches, a fastball, curveball and changeup. The fastball is his best pitch, registering in the mid-90s, and the other two pitches have the potential to be above average. Colon has no problem throwing strikes, a rare ability for a young pitcher. He eventually should become an impact pitcher, either a No. 1 starter or a dominating closer, at the major league level.

WEAKNESSES: Outside of his health—and the elbow appears to be fine—there are no question marks about Colon. He can improve the consistency of his breaking pitch. He doesn't have the height of a prototype power pitcher and lacks experience, but neither shortcoming has held him back.

FUTURE: Assuming the elbow problem doesn't flare up in training camp, Colon will likely skip a level and begin the season at Triple-A Buffalo. If not earlier, he should be able to join Cleveland's rotation in 1997.

— By Jim Ingraham

MINOR LEAGUE MENTIONS BY BA

YEAR	TOP 100	ORG RANKING	LEAGUE RANKING	BEST TOOLS
1995			No. 1: Carolina	**CAR:** Best Pitching Prospect, Best Fastball
1996	No. 15	No. 1: Indians	No. 8: Eastern	**EL:** Best Pitching Prospect, Best Fastball
1997	No. 14	No. 2: Indians		

DAVID CONE, RHP

BIOGRAPHY

PROPER NAME: David Brian Cone. **BORN:** January 2, 1963 in Kansas City, Mo.
HT: 6-1. **WT:** 190. **BATS:** L. **THROWS:** R. **SCHOOL:** Rockhurst HS, Kansas City, Mo.
FIRST PRO CONTRACT: Selected by Royals in third round (74th overall) of 1981 draft;
signed June 10, 1981.

KANSAS CITY ROYALS TOP 10 PROSPECTS FOR 1985

Knee surgery forced Cone to miss 1983 and created concern about how well he could bounce back after a long layoff at such an early stage of his career.

The questions were answered in a hurry. Don't worry about the 8-12 record and 4.28 ERA or even the 114 walks. The stat to consider in evaluating Cone's return is that he led the Memphis team with 179 innings pitched, and then had the second-lowest earned run average in the Florida Instructional League.

The knee never bothered him. He did appear to tire late in the season at Memphis, but was strong again for the FIL. This will be a big season for Cone to show that as well as being physically sound, he can regain command of his pitches. He has a plus fastball and adequate breaking pitches.

— By Tracy Ringolsby

KANSAS CITY ROYALS TOP 10 PROSPECTS FOR 1986

After missing the 1983 season because of a major knee surgery, Cone has proven durable the last two years. He also showed that he still had the 90-plus fastball that led the Royals to make Cone a fourth-round selection in the 1981 draft, despite the fact his high school did not have a baseball team.

But he continued to struggle with control problems (207 walks in 338 innings), although it appears everything came together during the winter. Pitching in Puerto Rico, Cone had a 1-5 record, but his ERA was 2.26, and more importantly, in 56 innings he cut his walks to 27 while striking out 45.

— By Tracy Ringolsby

MINOR LEAGUE MENTIONS BY BA

YEAR	TOP 100	ORG RANKING	LEAGUE RANKING	BEST TOOLS
1983		No. 6: Royals		
1984				
1985		No. 9: Royals		
1986		No. 3: Royals		AA: Best Fastball, Best Reliever

JOHNNY CUETO, RHP

BIOGRAPHY

PROPER NAME: Johnny Cueto.
BORN: February 15, 1986 in San Pedro de Macoris, Dominican Republic.
HT: 5-11. **WT:** 229. **BATS:** R. **THROWS:** R.
FIRST PRO CONTRACT: Signed as international free agent by Reds, March 16, 2004.

CINCINNATI REDS TOP 10 PROSPECTS FOR 2007

Cueto was the first player the Reds signed in the Dominican after revitalizing their nearly dormant Latin American scouting program. In his first extended taste of full-season ball, he went 15-3, 3.00 and allowed just one run in his final 30 innings in high Class A.

The 5-foot-10, 192- pounder doesn't look like he has a big arm, but Cueto throws a 92-94 mph fastball that touches 96 mph. He does so with a relatively free and easy high three-quarters delivery, and he commands his heat to both sides of the plate. During spring training, former Reds ace Mario Soto taught Cueto a changeup that quickly became a major league average pitch with tailing life. He also throws a slider that overmatches hitters at times.

Cueto's size doesn't lend itself to durability, but Cincinnati believes he'll be able to remain a starter. He has long arms that give him good leverage, so he doesn't wear himself out by throwing hard. He needs to get more consistent with his secondary pitches.

While he likes to challenge hitters up in the zone, that won't work as well at higher levels. He could open 2007 in Double-A at age 21.

— By J.J. Cooper

MINOR LEAGUE MENTIONS BY BA

YEAR	TOP 100	ORG RANKING	LEAGUE RANKING	BEST TOOLS
2006			**No. 12:** Midwest **No. 14:** Florida State	
2007		**No. 4:** Reds	**No. 5:** Florida State **No. 4:** Southern	
2008	No. 34	**No. 4:** Reds		

JACOB deGROM, RHP

BIOGRAPHY

PROPER NAME: Jacob Anthony deGrom. **BORN:** June 19, 1988 in De Leon Springs, Fla.
HT: 6-4. **WT:** 180. **BATS:** L. **THROWS:** R. **SCHOOL:** Stetson.
FIRST PRO CONTRACT: Selected by Mets in ninth round (272nd overall) of 2010 draft;
signed June 12, 2010.

NEW YORK METS TOP 10 PROSPECTS FOR 2014

DeGrom began his college career as the starting shortstop for Stetson before transitioning to the mound as a junior, first serving as closer before moving into the rotation down the stretch in 2010. He has completed four levels of the full-season minors in two years, after missing the entire 2011 season while rehabbing from Tommy John surgery he had the previous fall.

DeGrom succeeds by pounding the zone and showing a clean arm action and bulldog mentality. He threw nearly two-thirds of his pitches for strikes in 2013, though he would benefit form expanding the zone and getting batters to chase when he gets ahead in the count. He sits at 92-94 mph with plus sinking life, and he can rear back for 98 when he needs it. DeGrom made progress with a straight changeup this season, giving him a good weapon against lefties, though he misses more bats against righties with a fastball and slurvy breaking ball. He's working on improving the rotation and bite of his breaking ball.

After logging a combined 148 innings in 2013, deGrom has put his surgery completely behind him. An offseason addition to the 40-man roster, he likely will begin 2014 at Triple-A Las Vegas, flying standby for the big league rotation. He has a ceiling as a No. 4 starter or better.

— By Matt Eddy

MINOR LEAGUE MENTIONS BY BA

YEAR	TOP 100	ORG RANKING	LEAGUE RANKING	BEST TOOLS
2013		**No. 11:** Mets		
2014		**No. 10:** Mets		

CARLOS DELGADO, 1B

BIOGRAPHY

PROPER NAME: Carlos Juan Delgado. **BORN:** June 25, 1972 in Aguadilla, Puerto Rico.
HT: 6-3. **WT:** 245. **BATS:** L. **THROWS:** R. **SCHOOL:** Aguadilla, Puerto Rico.
FIRST PRO CONTRACT: Signed as international free agent by Blue Jays, Oct. 9, 1988.

TORONTO BLUE JAYS TOP 10 PROSPECTS FOR 1994

BACKGROUND: Singed as a gangly 16-year-old, Delgado spent his first two years in pro ball as a DH. After two years, he assumed full-time catching duty and quickly began to show power. He has 55 home runs the past two seasons and has at least 100 RBIs and a .300 average in each of those years.

STRENGTHS: Delgado has big-time power potential and he'll find a spot in the middle of a lineup. Capable of driving the ball to all fields, he has shown impressive discipline, drawing 102 walks in 1993.

WEAKNESSES: Learning the defensive art of catching has been a slow process for Delgado, but he made marked improvement in the second half of 1993. He has a strong arm, and as he matured the coordination has started to come. Still, he may not be a major league catcher.

FUTURE: Delgado has proven himself in the minors and is ready for the big leagues. He might not get a chance until midseason.

— **By Tim Pearrell**

MINOR LEAGUE MENTIONS BY BA

YEAR	TOP 100	ORG RANKING	LEAGUE RANKING	BEST TOOLS
1990			**No. 4:** New York-Penn	
1991		**No. 6:** Blue Jays	**No. 3:** South Atlantic	
1992	No. 67	**No. 5:** Blue Jays	**No. 1:** Florida State	**FSL:** Best Hitter, Best Power
1993	No. 4	**No. 1:** Blue Jays	**No. 2:** Southern	**SL:** Best Hitter, Best Power
1994	No. 5	**No. 2:** Blue Jays	**No. 3:** International	
1995			**No. 7:** International	

ERIC GAGNE, RHP

BIOGRAPHY

PROPER NAME: Eric Serge Gagne. **BORN:** January 7, 1976 in Montreal, Canada.
HT: 6-0. **WT:** 240. **BATS:** R. **THROWS:** R. **SCHOOL:** Seminole State (Okla.) JC
FIRST PRO CONTRACT: Signed as nondrafted free agent by Dodgers, July 26, 1995.

LOS ANGELES DODGERS TOP 10 PROSPECTS FOR 2000

BACKGROUND: Gagne, a member of the Canadian national junior team, was passed over in the 1995 draft and signed that summer. He missed the 1997 season after Tommy John surgery. He rebounded to lead all of Double-A in strikeouts and fewest hits per nine innings in 1999.

STRENGTHS: Gagne has a long, fluid three-quarters arm action, lending heavy sink to his 90-92 mph fastball. His changeup, an outstanding pitch he uses to close out hitters, gets similar sinking action from the same release point. The Dodgers describe Gagne's demeanor as tough, though opponents lean toward mean.

WEAKNESSES: Gagne's curveball lags behind his fastball and change. He had eye surgery following the season to correct problems that forced him to wear heavy goggles on the mound.

FUTURE: The previous regime didn't consider Gagne a prospect, but his performance in 1999 changed that. He is likely to start 2000 in the Dodgers rotation.

— **By David Rawnsley**

MINOR LEAGUE MENTIONS BY BA

YEAR	TOP 100	ORG RANKING	LEAGUE RANKING	BEST TOOLS
1999			**No. 6:** Texas	
2000	No. 49	**No. 2:** Dodgers		

NOMAR GARCIAPARRA, SS

BIOGRAPHY

PROPER NAME: Anthony Nomar Garciaparra. **BORN:** July 23, 1973 in Whittier, Calif.
HT: 6-0. **WT:** 165. **BATS:** R. **THROWS:** R. **SCHOOL:** Georgia Tech.
FIRST PRO CONTRACT: Selected by Red Sox in first round (12th overall) of 1994 draft;
signed July 20, 1994.

BOSTON RED SOX TOP 10 PROSPECTS FOR 1997

BACKGROUND: Garciaparra has become a better player than the Red Sox bargained for when they gave him $895,000 to sign in 1994. As the only true freshman ever to play for the U.S. Olympic team, he was a defensive whiz but mediocre at the plate. He became an accomplished college hitter at Georgia Tech, then added power to his game as a pro.

STRENGTHS: Garciaparra isn't flashy a la Rey Ordonez, but he's solid. Likewise his arm isn't a gun, but it's good enough and Garciaparra has a quick release. Boston initially hoped that he would become a No. 2 hitter, but he may have more bat that that. He worked out diligently last offseason, adding 15 pounds of muscle, and showed a previously undiscovered ability to loft balls. He now projects as being able to hit at least 10-15 homers per season, a huge bonus for such a strong defensive shortstop. Garciaparra can steal bases as well, having swiped 35 in Double-A in 1995 before injuries slowed him in 1996.

WEAKNESSES: Garciaparra has a bit of an uppercut to his swing, which big league pitchers began to exploit soon after his recall. But he made some adjustments and in his final six games he hit three homers, including an opposite-field shot over the Fenway Park bullpens.

FUTURE: Garciaparra claimed the Boston shortstop job with his late-season performance, moving incumbent John Valentin to third. He shouldn't relinquish it any time soon.

— **By Jim Callis**

MINOR LEAGUE MENTIONS BY BA

YEAR	TOP 100	ORG RANKING	LEAGUE RANKING	BEST TOOLS
1995	No. 22	**No. 1:** Red Sox	**No. 4:** Eastern	**EL:** Best Baserunner, Best Defensive SS
1996	No. 36	**No. 4:** Red Sox	**No. 1:** International	
1997	No. 10	**No. 1:** Red Sox		

JASON GIAMBI, 1B

BIOGRAPHY

PROPER NAME: Jason Gilbert Giambi. **BORN:** January 8, 1971 in West Covina, Calif.
HT: 6-3. **WT:** 240. **BATS:** L. **THROWS:** R. **SCHOOL:** Long Beach State.
FIRST PRO CONTRACT: Selected by the Athletics in second round (58th overall) of 1992 draft;
signed July 3, 1992.

CALIFORNIA LEAGUE TOP 10 PROSPECTS FOR 1993

Like Calvin Murray, a 1992 U.S. Olympian, Giambi started strong but was sidelined by a thumb injury for most of the second half. He has good hitting ability, excellent plate discipline (73 walks, 47 strikeouts) and was named the league's best defensive third baseman.

"He's a good contact hitter with occasional power," (Stockton Ports manager Lamar) Johnson said. "He did a good job against us at third."

— **By Maureen Delany**

OAKLAND ATHLETICS TOP 10 PROSPECTS FOR 1995

BACKGROUND: The 1992 Olympian has shown just about everything to make an offensive player offensive, most notably a .318 average after moving to Triple-A in '94.

STRENGTHS: Despite only 10 home runs in '94 and 16 the previous season, Giambi is considered a legitimate power source. Thumb and hand injuries have cut into his power. He also is probably the A's best potential average hitter. He could hit .300 in the big leagues with a high on-base percentage.

WEAKNESSES: All that separates Giambi from the majors is defense. He has shown improvement as he has moved through the system, but made 19 errors in 89 games at third base in 1994.

FUTURE: Giambi is almost ready offensively. If his glove work has improved, he could win the third-base job in spring training. More likely, he will spend the year at Triple-A Edmonton.

— **By Casey Tefertiller**

MINOR LEAGUE MENTIONS BY BA				
YEAR	TOP 100	ORG RANKING	LEAGUE RANKING	BEST TOOLS
1993			No. 9: California	
1994				
1995		No. 4: Athletics		

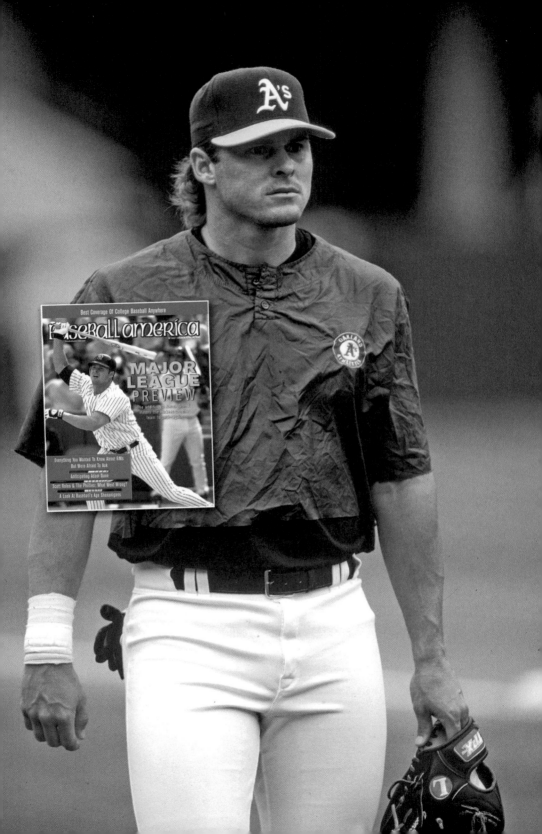

TOM GLAVINE, LHP

BIOGRAPHY

PROPER NAME: Thomas Michael Glavine. **BORN:** March 25, 1966 in Concord, Mass.
HT: 6-0. **WT:** 205. **BATS:** L. **THROWS:** L. **SCHOOL:** Billerica (Mass.) HS.
FIRST PRO CONTRACT: Selected by Braves in second round (47th overall) of 1984 draft;
signed June 22, 1984.

ATLANTA BRAVES TOP 10 PROSPECTS FOR 1986

Glavine defies logic. He really is 20; he really has concentrated on baseball as his No. 1 sport for only a year and a half; he really is a lefthander.

Just the same, he already is a pretty polished young pitcher who has outstanding composure, command of four pitches and the ability to throw as hard as he needs to against certain hitters in certain situations. It is a sinking fastball that Glavine already realizes he has to run in on hitters — lefthanded or righthanded — to succeed.

Check out the ratios from his first full pro season at Sumter: 169 innings, 114 hits, 73 walks and 174 strikeouts.

The Braves' second pick in June, 1984, Glavine turned down a college scholarship to play hockey and a pro hockey offer from the Los Angeles Kings, who drafted him in the fourth round of the NHL draft. The hockey background is obvious in the tenacity with which Glavine approaches pitching. He doesn't give in or get down when things go bad. He has that confidence that he can get out of the mess.

He combines the athletic ability and attitude along with the intelligence to learn quickly from instruction and mistakes. He was selected the Boston-area prep athlete and academic athlete of the year as a junior and senior — the only athlete to receive both honors in the same year.

— **By Tracy Ringolsby**

MINOR LEAGUE MENTIONS BY BA

YEAR	TOP 100	ORG RANKING	LEAGUE RANKING	BEST TOOLS
1985		No. 3: Braves		
1986		No. 2: Braves	No. 2: Southern	
1987		No. 2: Braves		

BaseBall america

FAB FORE!
TOM GLAVINE, STEVE AVERY
JOHN SMOLTZ & GREG MADDUX:
TERRORS ON THE MOUND
AND ON THE LINKS
BASEBALL'S
BEST AT
16 OTHER
SPORTS

TOP 25 COLLEGE PROSPECTS
BRAVES: TOO MUCH TALENT?
COLORADO SILVER BULLETS
MINOR LEAGUE PREVIEWS
TODD VAN POPPEL
ESPN'S PETER GAMMONS

PAUL GOLDSCHMIDT, 1B

BIOGRAPHY

PROPER NAME: Paul Edward Goldschmidt. **BORN:** September 10, 1987 in Wilmington, Del.
HT: 6-3. **WT:** 225. **BATS:** R. **THROWS:** R. **SCHOOL:** Texas State.
FIRST PRO CONTRACT: Selected by D-backs in 8th round (246th overall) of 2009 draft;
signed June 14, 2009.

ARIZONA DIAMONDBACKS TOP 30 PROSPECTS FOR 2011

Goldschmidt has a proven track record as a power hitter. He set a school record with 36 career home runs at Texas State, after first coming to scouts' attention in 2006, when he and Kyle Drabek (now the Blue Jays' top prospect) led The Woodlands (Texas) High to the national championship.

He led the Rookie-level Pioneer League in homers (18) and slugging percentage (.638) in his debut season, then jumped two levels to high Class A and topped the California League in doubles (42), home runs (35) and slugging (.606) en route to winning the MVP award. He also struck out 161 times, which some scouts see as an indication that he may struggle against better pitching as he moves higher in the system.

There's no denying Goldschmidt's legitimate power to all fields, and his supporters believe he has a swing path that will allow him to improve as a hitter. He was especially dangerous against lefthanders last year, batting .413/.453/.860 with 16 homers in just 143 at-bats, so even those who don't believe in him as a regular in the big leagues believe he can at least have a solid career as a platoon player.

His defense right now is adequate, and he has the potential to be an average major league first baseman because he's rangy for his size. His speed is well below-average, so he'll have to make it as a first baseman or DH. Goldschmidt will move up to Double A, where he'll be tested by better pitching.

— **By Bill Mitchell**

MINOR LEAGUE MENTIONS BY BA

YEAR	TOP 100	ORG RANKING	LEAGUE RANKING	BEST TOOLS
2010		No. 13: D-backs	No. 17: California	CAL: Best Power
2011		No. 11: D-backs	No. 3: Southern	SL: Best Hitter, Best Power, Best Strike-Zone Judgment, Best Defensive 1B, Most Exciting Player

JUAN GONZALEZ, OF

BIOGRAPHY

PROPER NAME: Juan Alberto Gonzalez. **BORN:** October 20, 1969 in Arecibo, Puerto Rico.
HT: 6-3. **WT:** 220. **BATS:** R. **THROWS:** R. **SCHOOL:** Vega Baja, Puerto Rico.
FIRST PRO CONTRACT: Signed as international free agent by Rangers, May 30, 1986.

TEXAS RANGERS TOP 10 PROSPECTS FOR 1988

Gonzalez doesn't have the dominating type of stats that one might expect, but it must be remembered that in the South Atlantic League last year he played at 17, younger than any other regular in the league and a good four to five years younger the bulk of the SAL players.

Just the same, the native of Puerto Rico who signed with the Rangers in 1986 put together a solid season, leading the Gastonia club in home runs and RBIs.

Still maturing physically and mentally, Gonzalez has excellent bat speed and a plus arm. He could play any of the outfield positions, but seems most comfortable in left field, where he is way above average in throwing strength.

More than anything, Gonzalez has to grow up emotionally. He takes every at-bat personally, and when he doesn't have instant success he gets down on himself. He'll fail to run out pop ups, not out of laziness, but frustration, and has to learn that a player of his ability is going to have every step he takes watched closely by others.

— **By Tracy Ringolsby**

MINOR LEAGUE MENTIONS BY BA

YEAR	TOP 100	ORG RANKING	LEAGUE RANKING	BEST TOOLS
1987		**No. 6:** Rangers	**No. 10:** South Atlantic	**SAL:** Best Defensive OF
1988		**No. 1:** Rangers		
1989		**No. 3:** Rangers	**No. 4:** Texas	**TL:** Best OF Arm
1990		**No. 1:** Rangers	**No. 1:** American Association	**AA:** Best Hitter, Best Power, Best OF Arm

Licey Rolls To The Winterball I Championship

Difficult Delivery: The Birth Of Zebulon's Ballpark

Baseball america

"Baseball News You Can't Get Anywhere Else"

March 10-24, 1991

Price: $2.95 ($3.95 In Canada)

Now In Our 11th Year

LEFT OUT IN THE COLD
THE BEST ROOKIES AREN'T ROOKIES

OUR ANNUAL ROOKIE RANKINGS
MO KNOWS BASEBALL
RED SOX FIRST BASEMAN MAURICE VAUGHN
PREPARES TO TAKE ON THE GREEN MONSTER

DWIGHT GOODEN, RHP

BIOGRAPHY

PROPER NAME: Dwight Eugene Gooden. **BORN:** November 16, 1964 in Tampa, Fla.
HT: 6-3. **WT:** 210. **BATS:** R. **THROWS:** R. **SCHOOL:** Hillsborough HS, Tampa.
FIRST PRO CONTRACT: Selected by Mets in first round (fifth overall) of 1982 draft;
signed June 10, 1982.

NEW YORK METS TOP 10 PROSPECTS FOR 1984

One of four hot pitching prospects to come out of the Tampa amateur program, Gooden moved to the head of the class in 1983. His first full pro season was remarkable. After going 19-4 with a 2.50 ERA and striking out 300 in 191 innings at Lynchburg, he was given a promotion to Tidewater for the AAA World Series and pitched a four-hitter, earning Baseball America Minor League Player of the Year honors. And all before he even turned 19.

There won't be many more birthdays to celebrate before Gooden celebrates his arrival in the big leagues. He throws between 90 and 95 mph and he's got an outstanding curveball.

"You see guys strike out a lot of batters with one exceptional pitch (at lower levels of the minor leagues)," Mets farm director Steve Schryver said, "but he'll blow hitters away with the fastball and then get them with the great curveball."

But there's more to Gooden than his arm. There's his makeup. He has exceptional poise, and "a savvy that goes beyond his limited experience. He has the things that remind you of the old-time pitchers."

Before he's ready to make the final jump to the big leagues, he's going to have to get better command (112 walks and 121 hits last year) and could use some work on pickoff moves.

— **By Ron Morris**

MINOR LEAGUE MENTIONS BY BA

YEAR	TOP 100	ORG RANKING	LEAGUE RANKING	BEST TOOLS
1983		**No. 4:** Mets	**No. 1:** Carolina	
1984		**No. 1:** Mets		

ZACK GREINKE, RHP

BIOGRAPHY

PROPER NAME: Donald Zackary Greinke. **BORN:** October 21, 1983 in Orlando.
HT: 6-2. **WT:** 200. **BATS:** R. **THROWS:** R. **SCHOOL:** Apopka (Fla.) HS.
FIRST PRO CONTRACT: Selected by Royals in first round (sixth overall) of 2002 draft;
signed July 13, 2002.

KANSAS CITY ROYALS TOP 10 PROSPECTS FOR 2003

Greinke turned down a Clemson scholarship to sign with the Royals for a $2.475 million bonus as the sixth overall pick. Because the Royals had no instructional league and Greinke got in just 12 innings last summer, they sent him to pitch in the Puerto Rican League over the winter.

Despite his inexperience on the mound, Greinke commands four above-average pitches. His fastball sits between 91 and 93 mph, and he likes to move it in and out on hitters. He also has a slider with good tilt, along with a curveball and changeup. Because he has plenty of athleticism, a compact delivery and easy arm action, Greinke may increase his velocity as he progresses. If that happens, he would profile as a No. 1 starter.

Though he has four pitches, Greinke rarely uses all of them in a given outing. He usually has two working at a time and tends to stick with them. Because he barely pitched after signing, the biggest key for Greinke is to get experience in game situations and continue to build his arm strength. He needs to work on pitching down in the strike zone more. He also needs to improve the command of his secondary pitches.

The Royals considered Greinke the most polished prep arm in the 2002 draft. Based on his performance in Puerto Rico, where he had a 2.45 ERA in 26 innings, Greinke could start the season in high Class A. While Greinke's stuff isn't as overwhelming as 2001 first-rounder Colt Griffin's, he's a workaholic who studies hitters and figures to succeed with his intellect and command.

— **By Will Kimmey**

MINOR LEAGUE MENTIONS BY BA

YEAR	TOP 100	ORG RANKING	LEAGUE RANKING	BEST TOOLS
2003	No. 54	**No. 1:** Royals	**No. 1:** Carolina **No. 2:** Texas	**CAR:** Best Pitching Prospect, Best Control
2004	No. 14	**No. 1:** Royals		

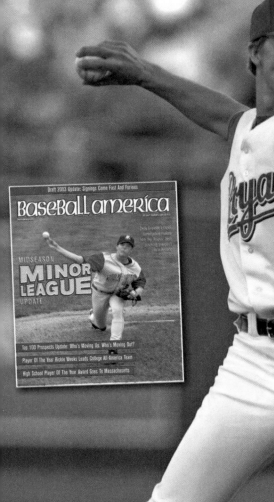

KEN GRIFFEY JR., OF

BIOGRAPHY

PROPER NAME: George Kenneth Griffey Jr. **BORN:** November 21, 1969 in Donora, Pa.
HT: 6-2. **WT:** 230. **BATS:** L. **THROWS:** L. **SCHOOL:** Archbishop Moeller HS, Cincinnati.
FIRST PRO CONTRACT: Selected by Mariners in first round (first overall) of 1987 draft;
signed June 2, 1987.

CALIFORNIA LEAGUE TOP 10 PROSPECTS FOR 1988

The managers surveyed agreed that Griffey, 19, has superstar skills.

"Griffey's an above-average guy in every category," said San Bernardino manager Ralph Dick. "He doesn't really have a weakness, and I think he's only going to get better and better."

"The only thing I'd do is not rush him," said Riverside's Tony Torchia. "Not making him pay his dues, necessarily, but letting him accumulate at-bats and have some success at each level."

— By Jim Alexander

SEATTLE MARINERS TOP 10 PROSPECTS FOR 1989

The No. 1 pick in 1987, Griffey might make it to the big leagues before his dad officially retires. Less than two years out of high school, he's almost ready.

His 1988 season was interrupted by a stress fracture in his back which cost him two months of playing time. But before the injury, he dominated the California League. When he returned, he was sent to Double-A, and survived, although it was obvious he was hurt by the idle time.

Griffey can do it all. He can hit for power (27 home runs in 458 minor league at-bats). He can run (49 stolen bases) He hits for average (composite .323). And he can play defense. His range and his arm are both above average.

— By Tracy Ringolsby

MINOR LEAGUE MENTIONS BY BA

YEAR	TOP 100	ORG RANKING	LEAGUE RANKING	BEST TOOLS
1987			**No. 1:** Northwest	
1988		**No. 1:** Mariners	**No. 1:** California	**CAL:** Best Hitter, Best Power, Best Defensive OF
1989		**No. 1:** Mariners		

VLADIMIR GUERRERO, OF

BIOGRAPHY

PROPER NAME: Vladimir Guerrero. **BORN:** February 9, 1975 in Nizao, Dominican Republic.
HT: 6-3. **WT:** 235. **BATS:** R. **THROWS:** R. **SCHOOL:** Nizao, Dominican Republic.
FIRST PRO CONTRACT: Signed as international free agent by Montreal Expos, March 1, 1993.

MONTREAL EXPOS TOP 10 PROSPECTS FOR 1996

BACKGROUND: Guerrero was signed in March 1993 by Expos international scouting director Fred Ferreira and was an immediate hit, batting .333 in the Dominican Summer League. He had one of the greatest half-season performances in the 10-year history of that league in 1994, hitting .424-12-35 in 25 games and prompting the Expos to move him to the Rookie-level Gulf Coast League to finish the season. His success continued into 1995 when he led the South Atlantic League in batting. His three-year career average: .341.

STRENGTHS: Guerrero is a potential all-star right fielder with two top-of-the-scale tools: power and arm strength. He was tall and skinny in 1994, but his bat speed increased in 1995 as his body matured. He began driving balls with power to all fields. Guerrero shows good strike-zone judgement for a player with his limited experience. He doesn't strike out much but still must learn to hit breaking balls with more conviction. Guerrero has learned to play all three outfield positions, which makes him a more skillful, well-rounded right fielder. Scouts praise his professional work ethic.

WEAKNESSES: Guerrero has above-average tools in all areas except speed. He has long, loping strides yet runs well enough to steal 15-20 bases per season.

FUTURE: The Explos plan to move Guerrero and several younger prospects as a group from Albany to Class A West Palm Beach in 1996. But they expect Guerrero to emerge from the pack and reach Double-A before the end of the season. He should be in Montreal by 1998 and become a player who can excel in all phases of the game.

— By Allan Simpson

MINOR LEAGUE MENTIONS BY BA

YEAR	TOP 100	ORG RANKING	LEAGUE RANKING	BEST TOOLS
1994			**No. 4:** Gulf Coast	
1995	No. 85	**No. 5:** Expos	**No. 2:** South Atlantic	**SAL:** Best OF Arm
1996	No. 9	**No. 1:** Expos	**No. 1:** Eastern	**EL:** Best Hitter, Best Power, Best Defensive OF, Best OF Arm, Most Exciting Player
1997	No. 2	**No. 1:** Expos		

ROY HALLADAY, RHP

BIOGRAPHY

PROPER NAME: Harry Leroy Halladay. **BORN:** May 14, 1977 in Denver.
HT: 6-6. **WT:** 225. **BATS:** R. **THROWS:** R. **SCHOOL:** Arvada (Colo.) West HS.
FIRST PRO CONTRACT: Selected by Blue Jays in first round (17th overall) of 1995 draft;
signed June 30, 1995.

TORONTO BLUE JAYS TOP 10 PROSPECTS FOR 1998

BACKGROUND: The youngest player in the Triple-A International League after his midseason promotion, Halladay finished 1997 strong and had two shutouts. He is a true athlete with the tall, lean pitcher's body that scouts seek. Another in the long line of Colorado pitchers tutored by pitching guru Bus Campbell (now a Blue Jays scout) Halladay not only was a star on the mound in high school but also finished third in the state cross-country meet in his senior year. Halladay continued to show marked improvement this winter in Venezuela.

STRENGTHS: Halladay's fastball ranges from a low of 92 mph to a high of 97 mph but is consistently in the 93-95 range. He has good command of the pitch and cuts it effectively for movement. Though he is a young power pitcher, he has walked only 126 batters in 377 professional innings. Like many of Campbell's pupils, Halladay dabbles with a knuckle-curve.

WEAKNESSES: The biggest challenge facing Halladay is merely getting experience. He reached Triple-A in just his second full pro season. Once Halladay finds consistency with his knuckle-curve, he should be ready to make his move to the big leagues.

FUTURE: Halladay will return to Triple-A Syracuse to open the 1998 season and likely will spend the full season there. But he could arrive faster if he begins to master the knuckle-curve.

— **By Tracy Ringolsby**

MINOR LEAGUE MENTIONS BY BA

YEAR	TOP 100	ORG RANKING	LEAGUE RANKING	BEST TOOLS
1995			**No. 5:** Gulf Coast	
1996		**No. 6:** Blue Jays	**No. 3:** Florida State	
1997	No. 23	**No. 1:** Blue Jays	**No. 5:** International	**IL:** Best Fastball
1998	No. 38	**No. 1:** Blue Jays	**No. 3:** International	**IL:** Best Fastball
1999	No. 12	**No. 1:** Blue Jays		

COLE HAMELS, LHP

BIOGRAPHY

PROPER NAME: Colbert Michael Hamels. **BORN:** December 27, 1983 in San Diego, Calif.
HT: 6-4. **WT:** 205. **BATS:** L. **THROWS:** L. **SCHOOL:** Rancho Bernardo HS, San Diego.
FIRST PRO CONTRACT: Selected by Phillies in first round (17th overall) of 2002 draft;
signed Aug. 28, 2002.

PHILADELPHIA PHILLIES TOP 10 PROSPECTS FOR 2004

Hamels had nothing but question marks entering his pro career and has provided only exclamation points since signing. He ranked as one of the top pitchers in the 2002 draft, but a broken humerus in his left arm caused him to miss his junior season at Rancho Bernardo High and slip to the 17th pick.

Hamels should have three above-average pitches when he reaches the majors. He already shows plus command of a fastball that sits between 89-92 mph with plenty of movement. He can reach back for more when he needs it, topping out at 94. His best pitch might be his plus-plus changeup, which was neck-and-neck with Ryan Madson's as the best in the organization and possibly the minors. Hamels displays exceptional control of his changeup at such a young age, and it drops and fades away from hitters. Hamels shows a businesslike demeanor, with no great highs or lows. He's a great athlete, allowing him to repeat his delivery, hold runners and field his position well. Hamels' curveball should become a third plus pitch, and its movement is already there.

He just needs to develop more consistency with the curve. His overall command and control are advanced for his age—and ahead of where Floyd and Brett Myers were at similar stages in their development—but he can continue to improve it as he progresses. Hamels hasn't experienced any repercussions from his high school arm injury. A pulled muscle in his right shoulder blade caused the Phillies to remove him from the trials for Team USA's Olympic qualifying squad. The minor injury isn't a long-term concern, and he should begin 2004 on schedule by returning to high Class A Clearwater.

— **By Will Kimmey**

MINOR LEAGUE MENTIONS BY BA

YEAR	TOP 100	ORG RANKING	LEAGUE RANKING	BEST TOOLS
2003		**No. 5:** Phillies	**No. 3:** South Atlantic	**SAL:** Best Breaking Pitch
2004	No. 17	**No. 1:** Phillies		
2005	No. 71	**No. 3:** Phillies		
2006	No. 68	**No. 1:** Phillies		

MIKE HAMPTON, LHP

BIOGRAPHY

PROPER NAME: Michael William Hampton. **BORN:** September 9, 1972 in Brooksville, Fla.
HT: 5-10. **WT:** 195. **BATS:** R. **THROWS:** L. **SCHOOL:** Crystal River (Fla.) HS.
FIRST PRO CONTRACT: Selected by Mariners in sixth round (161st overall) of 1990 draft;
signed June 4, 1990.

CALIFORNIA LEAGUE TOP 10 PROSPECTS FOR 1992

Hampton is a finesse pitcher with an excellent curveball and changeup. At 5-foot-10, 180 pounds, he isn't overpowering but has good control. He went 13-8, 3.12, striking out 132 in 170 innings.

"He's a gamer," San Bernardino manager Ivan DeJesus said. "That's what keeps him in there. He has a good breaking ball and when he's in a spot, he has a good fastball. He's not afraid to throw the curveball at a 3-1 or 3-2 count."

— **By Maureen Delany**

SEATTLE MARINERS TOP 10 PROSPECTS FOR 1993

Hampton might rank higher in this survey if he didn't stand two inches short of six feet. The Mariners, though, think he eventually will be a durable major league starter.

Hampton throws with slightly above-average velocity and works both sides of the plate with his fastball. He is gaining command of a curve with some slider-type action, and has an effective changeup. When his pitches are in sync, Hampton can control a game with ground balls and strikeouts.

Though he's made only two starts above Class A, Hampton could be ready for a major league audition sometime in 1993. Aggressive and confident, he competes fiercely and maintains composure under adversity.

— **By Ken Leiker**

MINOR LEAGUE MENTIONS BY BA

YEAR	TOP 100	ORG RANKING	LEAGUE RANKING	BEST TOOLS
1992		**No. 4:** Mariners	**No. 5:** California	
1993		**No. 7:** Mariners		

BRYCE HARPER, OF

BIOGRAPHY

PROPER NAME: Bryce Aron Max Harper. **BORN:** October 16, 1992 in Las Vegas.
HT: 6-3. **WT:** 220. **BATS:** L. **THROWS:** R. **SCHOOL:** JC of Southern Nevada.
FIRST PRO CONTRACT: Selected by Nationals in first round (first overall) of 2010 draft;
signed August 16, 2010.

WASHINGTON NATIONALS TOP 10 PROSPECTS FOR 2011

Harper was already established as a phenom before Sports Illustrated dubbed him Baseball's Chosen One on its cover in June 2009—when he had just completed sophomore year in high school and was 16 years old. Since then, he has been confronted with gargantuan expectations everywhere he has gone, yet he has managed to exceed even the loftiest projections.

Harper's raw tools are freakish. His power rates as a legitimate 80 tool on the 20-80 scouting scale. There are plenty of stories and videos of him hitting 500-foot homers, and he has the ability to easily backspin the ball over the fence to any part of the park. Harper is incredibly intense and aggressive in all phases of the game, including at the plate. Some scouts wonder if he'll hit for a high average because of his propensity to take huge swings, often with an exaggerated leg kick, and get jumpy at the plate. But at other times he shows a much quieter, more efficient swing. Those flashes, coupled with his uncanny hand-eye coordination and irreproachable work ethic, give other scouts reason to believe he'll eventually become more selective and produce for average as well as power. Harper has shown 95 mph heat off the mound in the past, and his accurate outfield arm gives him a second 80 tool. His slightly above-average speed plays up on the basepaths because he's extremely aggressive at taking the extra base. He's still refining his routes and reads in right field, but he has the athleticism and instincts to be a plus defender there.

The most hyped prospect in draft history, Harper has superstar potential, and it's hard to find an evaluator who thinks he'll fall short of that ceiling. A realistic big league ETA for Harper is 2013 when he'll be just 20.

— **By Aaron Fitt**

MINOR LEAGUE MENTIONS BY BA

YEAR	TOP 100	ORG RANKING	LEAGUE RANKING	BEST TOOLS
2011	No. 1	**No. 1:** Nationals	**No. 1:** South Atlantic **No. 1:** Eastern	**SAL:** Best Hitter, Best Power, Most Exciting Player
2012	No. 1	**No. 1:** Nationals		

FELIX HERNANDEZ, RHP

BIOGRAPHY

PROPER NAME: Felix Abraham Hernandez. **BORN:** April 8, 1986 in Valencia, Venezuela.
HT: 6-3. **WT:** 225. **BATS:** R. **THROWS:** R. **SCHOOL:** U.E. Jose Austre, Valencia, Venezuela.
FIRST PRO CONTRACT: Signed as international free agent by Mariners, July 4, 2002.

SEATTLE MARINERS TOP 10 PROSPECTS FOR 2004

The Mariners expected Hernandez to be good when they signed him for $710,000 in July 2002. But they didn't expect him to be this good, this fast.

Hernandez has scary upside. He'll open this season as a 17-year-old and he doesn't need to develop any more stuff. The only guy in the organization with a comparable arm is big leaguer Rafael Soriano. Hernandez has the best fastball in the system and commands his mid-90s heat well. He regularly touches 97 and could reach triple digits as his skinny frame fills out. Hernandez' curveball is also unparalleled among Mariners farmhands and gives him the possibility for two 70 pitches on the 20-80 scouting scale. Though he's young and can easily overpower hitters at the lower levels, he understands the value of a changeup and is developing a good one. He can pitch down in the strike zone or blow the ball by hitters upstairs. He has poise and mound presence beyond his years.

Hernandez just has to learn how to pitch. He needs to tweak his command and refine his pitches on the way to Seattle. Typical of a teenager with a lightning arm, he'll overthrow at times but should grow out of that. Arm problems would appear to be the only thing that could derail him from stardom, and Hernandez has been perfectly healthy so far. Seattle wants to move Hernandez slowly, but he may not let that happen. He's not going to need to spend a full season at each level and might need just two more years in the minors. It's easy to get overexcited about young pitchers, but Hernandez has the legitimate potential to become the best pitcher ever developed by the Mariners.

— **By Jim Callis**

MINOR LEAGUE MENTIONS BY BA

YEAR	TOP 100	ORG RANKING	LEAGUE RANKING	BEST TOOLS
2003			**No. 1:** Northwest	
2004	No. 30	**No. 1:** Mariners	**No. 1:** California **No. 1:** Texas	**CAL:** Best Pitching Prospect, Best Fastball, Best Breaking Pitch
2005	No. 2	**No. 1:** Mariners	**No. 1:** Pacific Coast	**PCL:** Best Pitching Prospect, Best Fastball, Best Breaking Pitch

TREVOR HOFFMAN, RHP

BIOGRAPHY

PROPER NAME: Trevor William Hoffman. **BORN:** October 13, 1967 in Bellflower, Calif.
HT: 6-0. **WT:** 220. **BATS:** R. **THROWS:** R. **SCHOOL:** Arizona.
FIRST PRO CONTRACT: Selected by the Reds in 11th round (290th overall) of 1989 draft;
signed June 9, 1989.

CINCINNATI REDS TOP 10 PROSPECTS FOR 1992

A career .227 hitter, Hoffman was on the verge of being released by the Reds after the 1990 season. He was spared only by Jim Lett, his manager at Charleston, who suggested that Hoffman be given one last chance—as a pitcher. Voila! Hoffman always had terrific arm strength, but the Reds never envisioned he would adapt to pitching almost overnight.

He showed rare command for someone who hadn't pitched in years, consistently throwing first-pitch strikes and dominating hitters at Cedar Rapids with a fastball clocked up to 95 mph. Hoffman has progressed so fast that some in the organization believe he has a chance to crack the big league staff in a setup role out of spring training.

— By Allan Simpson

TOP 10 LONGSHOT PROSPECTS FOR 1992

A shortstop with a weak bat, Hoffman turned to pitching last year as a last resort. It turned out that he had an outstanding fastball that was good enough for 20 saves last year, and possibly a role as a setup man in Cincinnati in 1992.

— By Jim Callis

MINOR LEAGUE MENTIONS BY BA

YEAR	TOP 100	ORG RANKING	LEAGUE RANKING	BEST TOOLS
1992		No. 8: Reds		

TIM HUDSON, RHP

BIOGRAPHY

PROPER NAME: Timothy Adam Hudson. **BORN:** July 14, 1975 in Columbus, Ga.
HT: 6-1. **WT:** 175. **BATS:** R. **THROWS:** R. **SCHOOL:** Auburn.
FIRST PRO CONTRACT: Selected by Athletics in sixth round (185th overall) of 1997 draft;
signed June 13, 1997.

OAKLAND ATHLETICS TOP 10 PROSPECTS FOR 1999

BACKGROUND: Hudson was a two-way star at Auburn, earning a spot on the All-America team as a utilityman his senior season after going 15-2, 2.97 on the mound and batting .396-18-95 as a center fielder. He put his bat away when he was drafted by the A's as a pitcher.

STRENGTHS: Around the A's front office, they call Hudson's fastball Super Sink. Not only does it drop, it darts as well. He knows how to use the pitch to induce a lot of ground balls. He also throws an excellent changeup, a satisfactory splitter and an occasional slider.

WEAKNESSES: Hudson is so skinny he can hide behind a fungo bat. The A's worry that he may lack stamina to endure the rigors of a full big league season. The slider also needs work and is not yet of major league caliber.

FUTURE: Hudson has a shot at a major league bullpen job this spring. If the A's decide to leave him as a starter, he will go to Midland or Vancouver.

— **By Casey Tefertiller**

PACIFIC COAST LEAGUE TOP TOP 10 PROSPECTS FOR 1999

Hudson shut up the ladder after going 10-9, 4.54 in Double-A last season in his first full pro season. He started back in Double-A and went 3-0, 0.50 before earning promotions to Triple-A and the majors, where he excelled.

"His stuff is electric," said Vancouver manager Mike Quade. "I don't think even our scouting director knew how good he was going to be so quickly."

The only thing the Athletics might need to do to help Hudson's development would be to increase his meal money. He's still pretty skinny.

— **By Peter Barrouquere and Laurence Miedema**

MINOR LEAGUE MENTIONS BY BA

YEAR	TOP 100	ORG RANKING	LEAGUE RANKING	BEST TOOLS
1999		No. 10: Athletics	No. 7: Pacific Coast	

DEREK JETER, SS

BIOGRAPHY

PROPER NAME: Derek Sanderson Jeter. **BORN:** June 26, 1974 in Pequannock, N.J.
HT: 6-3. **WT:** 195. **BATS:** R. **THROWS:** R. **SCHOOL:** Kalamazoo (Mich.) Central HS.
FIRST PRO CONTRACT: Selected by Yankees in first round (sixth overall) of 1992 draft;
signed June 27, 1992.

NEW YORK YANKEES TOP 10 PROSPECTS FOR 1993

Jeter received a $700,000 bonus from the Yankees last June, then struggled in all aspects of his game in the Rookie-level Gulf Coast League. He hit .202, was erratic in the field and only occasionally displayed his five-tool ability.

The Yankees aren't concerned with Jeter's slow start. They say he has no weaknesses. They also feel he's capable of following the same path as Chipper Jones, who struggled in his debut yet now ranks as the game's best prospect. Jones was the first high school player drafted in 1990, Jeter the first in 1992.

— **By Allan Simpson**

FLORIDA STATE LEAGUE TOP 10 PROSPECTS FOR 1994

Jeter, Baseball America's 1994 Minor League Player of the Year, has the complete package. He spent a half-season with Tampa and led the league in hitting before moving on to Double-A Albany and Triple-A Columbus. The FSL MVP could be the Yankees' shortstop next season.

He has basestealing speed and pop in his bat. Some say Jeter's defense is at least as good as Cal Ripken Jr.'s was at the same age (20).

"He does it all," one FSL manager said. "If he has a weakness, I didn't see it." Another skipper called Jeter a future superstar.

— **By Sean Kernan**

MINOR LEAGUE MENTIONS BY BA

YEAR	TOP 100	ORG RANKING	LEAGUE RANKING	BEST TOOLS
1993	No. 44	**No. 2:** Yankees	**No. 2:** South Atlantic	**SAL:** Best Defensive SS, Best INF Arm, Most Exciting Player
1994	No. 16	**No. 1:** Yankees	**No. 1:** Florida State **No. 3:** Eastern	**FSL:** Best Hitter, Best INF Arm, Most Exciting Player
1995	No. 4	**No. 2:** Yankees	**No. 3:** International	**IL:** Best Hitter, Most Exciting Player
1996	No. 6	**No. 2:** Yankees		

Baseball America

THE BASE PREVIEW OCTBER 16, 1994

PRIDE
OF THE
YANKEES

DEREK JETER
MINOR LEAGUE
PLAYER OF THE YEAR

MINOR LEAGUE
FINAL STATISTICS

ESPN'S PETER GAMMONS

DON BAYLOR, PHIL GARNER
FROM UNION ACTIVISTS
TO MANAGERS

RANDY JOHNSON, LHP

BIOGRAPHY

PROPER NAME: Randall David Johnson. **BORN:** September 10, 1963 in Walnut Creek, Ga.
HT: 6-10. **WT:** 225. **BATS:** R. **THROWS:** L. **SCHOOL:** Southern California.
FIRST PRO CONTRACT: Selected by Montreal Expos in second round (36th overall) of 1985
draft; signed June 9, 1985.

MONTREAL EXPOS TOP 10 PROSPECTS FOR 1987

Signed out of USC as a second-round pick in 1985, Johnson has the best fastball in the organization, consistently registering in the mid-90s range.

Once he was able to maintain a stable delivery, Johnson's control improved considerably last season (94 walks and 133 strikeouts in 120 innings). Working with only one dominant pitch, he limited hitters to a .211 average.

Johnson spent the fall in the Florida Instructional League working to develop a slider and changeup. The Expos saw enough progress that he will advance to Double-A as a starter, but his eventual role might be in short relief.

— **By Ken Leiker**

SOUTHERN LEAGUE TOP 10 PROSPECTS FOR 1987

Johnson, 24, was 11-8 with a 3.78 ERA and led the league in strikeouts with 163, utilizing a fastball consistently clocked in the 90s. But at 6-foot-10, he had problems with his control, 128 walks in 140 innings pitched.

"Has more potential than any pitcher in the league," (Birmingham manager Rico) Petrocelli said. "Has control problems, but can throw 93-plus ... It will take time ... but he can be a real good one. He'll either be a great one or one that will just never put it together — no in-between."

— **By Rubin Grant**

MINOR LEAGUE MENTIONS BY BA

YEAR	TOP 100	ORG RANKING	LEAGUE RANKING	BEST TOOLS
1986			No. 3: Florida State	FSL: Best Pitching Prospect, Best Fastball
1987		No. 3: Expos	No. 2: Southern	SL: Best Pitching Prospect, Best Fastball
1988	No. 1: Expos		No. 3: American Association	
1989		No. 2: Expos		

ANDRUW JONES, OF

BIOGRAPHY

PROPER NAME: Andruw Rudolf Jones. **BORN:** April 23, 1977 in Willemstad, Curacao.
HT: 6-1. **WT:** 225. **BATS:** R. **THROWS:** R. **SCHOOL:** St. Paulus, Willemstad, Curacao
FIRST PRO CONTRACT: Signed as international free agent by Braves, July 1, 1993.

APPALACHIAN LEAGUE TOP 10 PROSPECTS FOR 1994

Another 17-year-old making his debut, Jones jumped from the Rookie-level Gulf Coast League in midseason. He's a five-tool player whose best weapon is his speed, stealing bases and covering ground in the outfield. He also has a strong, accurate arm. Jones showed some ability to turn on fastballs and should hit for average with a bit of power. He can lay down a bunt when necessary.

— **By James Bailey**

ATLANTA BRAVES TOP 10 PROSPECTS FOR 1995

BACKGROUND: In his first year of pro ball, Jones was named the No. 2 prospect in the Appalachian League after making the jump from the Gulf Coast League, where he was ranked No. 3.

STRENGTHS: Jones is one of the most gifted athletes in the minor leagues. A true five-tool player, he's a burner who uses his speed and instincts in the outfield and on the bases. His arm is among the best in the organization.

WEAKNESSES: Jones simply needs to play. His lack of professional experience is the only thing keeping him from being an impact player at higher levels.

FUTURE: Jones should start 1995 at Class A Macon. No one in Atlanta would be surprised if he rises through the organization rapidly. They quietly compare him to Roberto Clemente.

— **By Bill Ballew**

MINOR LEAGUE MENTIONS BY BA

YEAR	TOP 100	ORG RANKING	LEAGUE RANKING	BEST TOOLS
1994			**No. 3:** Gulf Coast **No. 2:** Appalachian	
1995	No. 21	**No. 2:** Braves	**No. 1:** South Atlantic	**SAL:** Best Hitter, Best Power, Best Baserunner, Best Defensive OF, Most Exciting Player
1996	No. 1	**No. 1:** Braves	**No. 1:** Carolina **No. 1:** Southern	**CAR:** Best Hitter, Best Defensive OF, Most Exciting Player
1997	No. 1	**No. 1:** Braves		

CHIPPER JONES, 3B

BIOGRAPHY

PROPER NAME: Larry Wayne Jones. **BORN:** April 24, 1972 in DeLand, Fla.
HT: 6-4. **WT:** 210. **BATS:** B. **THROWS:** R. **SCHOOL:** Bolles HS, Jacksonville.
FIRST PRO CONTRACT: Selected by Braves in first round (first overall) of 1990 draft;
signed June 4, 1990.

ATLANTA BRAVES TOP 10 PROSPECTS FOR 1994

BACKGROUND: The youngest player in Triple-A in 1993, Jones continued to show why the Braves used the first overall pick in the 1990 draft to acquire his services. Handling another jump in classification for the third straight season, the immensely confident shortstop earned rookie-of-the-year honors in the International League and led a talented Richmond club in eight offensive categories.

STRENGTHS: Most young players' defensive skills reach major league standards before their offense catches up. Jones is an exception, wielding a potent stick that scouts believe will produce consistent .300-20-80 seasons in the majors. A natural line-drive hitter with exceptional bat control, Jones could resurrect the days of slugging third baseman if he continues to grow.

WEAKNESSES: Jones has good hands and a strong arm, yet was plagued by errors again in 1993. Many of his 43 errors either occurred late in games or after he made an error earlier, both of which could be remedied with stronger concentration. He was tried at second base in instructional league, but feels more comfortable on the left side of the infield.

FUTURE: Though he may begin the season back in Richmond, Jones will battle for a major league job in spring training and will play in Atlanta at some point in 1994.

— **By Bill Ballew**

MINOR LEAGUE MENTIONS BY BA

YEAR	TOP 100	ORG RANKING	LEAGUE RANKING	BEST TOOLS
1991	No. 49	**No. 2:** Braves	**No. 2:** South Atlantic	**SAL:** Best Infield Arm
1992	No. 4	**No. 1:** Braves	**No. 1:** Carolina **No. 1:** Southern	**CAR:** Best Defensive SS
1993	No. 1	**No. 1:** Braves	**No. 2:** International	
1994	No. 2	**No. 1:** Braves		
1995	No. 3	**No. 1:** Braves		

Baseball
america

**MAJOR
LEAGUE
PREVIEW**

GENERATION NEXT:
CHIPPER JONES
LEADS BASEBALL'S
NEW WAVE OF
REFRESHING STARS

GMs RANK THE
BIG LEAGUE TEAMS

THE CUBAN
PHENOMENON

TOM GLAVINE:
ATLANTA'S
OVERLOOKED ACE

FARM SYSTEM
EVALUATIONS:
LOS ANGELES
COMES OUT ON TOP

PHIL NEVIN:
FROM NO. 1 PICK
TO HUMBLE PIE

OLYMPIC NOTEBOOK

JEFF KENT, 2B

BIOGRAPHY

PROPER NAME: Jeffrey Franklin Kent. **BORN:** March 7, 1968 in Bellflower, Calif.
HT: 6-2. **WT:** 210. **BATS:** R. **THROWS:** R. **SCHOOL:** California.
FIRST PRO CONTRACT: Selected by Blue Jays in 20th round (523rd overall) of 1989 draft;
signed June 9, 1989.

TORONTO BLUE JAYS ORGANIZATIONAL REPORT FOR 1992

Jeff Kent wasn't surprised when he was sent to Triple-A at the end of spring training. He wasn't disappointed. He understood.

"I've got a smile on my face and I'm going to go down and work hard," he said. Kent made an impression during spring training when he batted .375.

Converted from a shortstop-third baseman to second base in 1990, Kent also showed a strong arm when he had a chance to play third in exhibition games. He didn't have to wait long for his call to the majors, as injuries meant Kent was called up two games into the major league season.

"I'm probably the most expendable player on this team" Kent said. "I won't be regretful if I am sent down. That's my role right now. But you never know."

His comments proved prophetic. The Jays may be regretful if the time comes to return Kent to Syracuse. When Kelly Gruber begged off with neck spasms against the Orioles, Kent took his place. In his first at-bat he doubled. In his second at-bat he hit the ball even harder but right at the third baseman.

As Gruber rested his neck, Kent had at least one hit in each of his first three games, including his first big league homer in a 12-6 rout of the Yankees.

Fans were beginning to wonder if Kent could play shortstop instead of the light-hitting Manuel Lee. Kent, who played shortstop at California says former Blue Jays infielder Garth Iorg, who coached at Class A Dunedin before managing at Rookie-level Medicine Hat, helped his conversion to second base.

"I respect him a lot," Kent said. "I never had a chance to play for him, but as a coach that half-season at Dunedin he taught me a lot about the mental part of the game. We're both Mormons. That doesn't mean everything in the world, but we respect each other because of that."

— By Larry Millson

MINOR LEAGUE MENTIONS BY BA

YEAR	TOP 100	ORG RANKING	LEAGUE RANKING	BEST TOOLS
1990				**FSL:** Best Defensive 2B

CLAYTON KERSHAW, LHP

BIOGRAPHY

PROPER NAME: Clayton Edward Kershaw. **BORN:** March 19, 1988 in Dallas, Texas.
HT: 6-4. **WT:** 228. **BATS:** L. **THROWS:** L. **SCHOOL:** Highland Park HS, University Park, Texas.
FIRST PRO CONTRACT: Selected by Dodgers in first round (seventh overall) of 2006 draft;
signed June 20, 2006.

LOS ANGELES DODGERS TOP 10 PROSPECTS FOR 2008

Kershaw blossomed into the best high school prospect in the 2006 draft after he gained velocity on his fastball and tightened his curveball. The Tigers were set to take him with the sixth overall pick before Andrew Miller unexpectedly fell in their laps, allowing Kershaw to drop one more spot to the Dodgers.

Kershaw pitches off a fastball that rests comfortably at 93-94 mph. He touched 99 a handful of times last summer. Kershaw's heater has late, riding life with explosive finish at the plate. His 71-77 mph curveball has hard 1-to-7 tilt from his high-three-quarters arm slot. He made strides with his changeup during the year, and it too grades as a third plus future offering. He generates his stuff with a loose, clean arm action. At 6-foot-3 and 210 pounds, he has an ideal pitcher's frame that exudes durability as well as athleticism. He eventually should pitch with above-average command, though he didn't show it in 2007.

Kershaw is a little slow to the plate, but is cognizant of baserunners. He employs a slide-step effectively and has a good pickoff move. The shape of his breaking ball is somewhat inconsistent, and he'll need to continue to work on sharpening his secondary pitches.

Kershaw offers a promising combination of front-of-the-rotation stuff and the work ethic to reach his ceiling as an ace. Some in the organization say his stuff is more advanced than Chad Billingsley's and Jonathan Broxton's at the same stage of their development. Now he has to apply the polish.

— **By Alan Matthews**

MINOR LEAGUE MENTIONS BY BA

YEAR	TOP 100	ORG RANKING	LEAGUE RANKING	BEST TOOLS
2006			**No. 1:** Gulf Coast	
2007	No. 24	**No. 2:** Dodgers	**No. 1:** Midwest	**MWL:** Best Pitching Prospect, Best Fastball
2008	No. 7	**No. 1:** Dodgers	**No. 1:** Southern	**SL:** Best Pitching Prospect, Best Fastball, Best Breaking Pitch

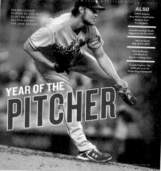

DALLAS KEUCHEL, LHP

BIOGRAPHY

PROPER NAME: Dallas Keuchel. **BORN:** January 1, 1988 in Tulsa, Okla.
HT: 6-3. **WT:** 205. **BATS:** L. **THROWS:** L. **SCHOOL:** Arkansas.
FIRST PRO CONTRACT: Selected by Astros in seventh round (221st overall) of 2009 draft;
signed June 24, 2009.

HOUSTON ASTROS TOP 30 PROSPECTS FOR 2012

Keuchel won 19 games in three seasons at Arkansas, leading the Razorbacks to the 2009 College World Series, and he's continued to win in pro ball, even in an Astros system all too accustomed to losing. He was the only Houston farmhand to reach 10 victories in 2011.

He's a rare lefthanded sinkerballer who pitches inside even though his fastball sits at only 84-87 mph. He has touched 90-91 in the past but generally relies on movement and location. Keuchel mixes up his tempo, at times adding a hitch to his delivery, and also employs a slow curveball to keep hitters off balance. His best pitch is a sinking changeup that has better action than his fastball and grades as solid or better. Righthanders batted .255 against him last year, while lefties hit .305.

His overall package compares best to finesse southpaws such as Zane Smith or Doug Davis. Keuchel is extremely durable, working 174 innings in 2010 and 189 last year (including his time in the Arizona Fall League). A potential back-of-the-rotation starter or middle reliever, he'll have to keep proving himself one level at a time. He'll start 2012 back in Triple-A, where he was rocked in four of his seven late-season starts.

— By John Manuel

MINOR LEAGUE MENTIONS BY BA

YEAR	TOP 100	ORG RANKING	LEAGUE RANKING	BEST TOOLS
2010		No. 24: Astros		CAR: Best Changeup
2011		No. 23: Astros		TL: Best Changeup
2012		No. 21: Astros		

CRAIG KIMBREL, RHP

BIOGRAPHY

PROPER NAME: Craig Michael Kimbrel. **BORN:** May 28, 1988 in Huntsville, Ala.
HT: 6-0. **WT:** 210. **BATS:** R. **THROWS:** R. **SCHOOL:** Wallace State (Ala.) JC.
FIRST PRO CONTRACT: Selected by Braves in third round (96th overall) of 2008 draft;
signed June 6, 2008.

ATLANTA BRAVES TOP 10 PROSPECTS FOR 2010

Kimbrel turned down $125,000 as a Braves 33rd-round pick in 2007 before signing for $391,000 as a third-rounder a year later. He overcame a slow start at high Class A Myrtle Beach—he had 18 walks and a 10.97 ERA in 11 innings—to save 18 games and rank second among minor league relievers with 15.5 strikeouts per nine innings.

Kimbrel has the stuff and mentality to be a big league closer. He aggressively challenges hitters with his plus-plus fastball, which sits at 93-95 mph, touches 98 and has nasty life. He also throws an above-average breaking ball that he calls a curveball but looks more like a slider. He flashes a deceptive changeup, though he rarely used it in 2009.

Kimbrel needs to pitch inside more often with his fastball. Though he showed marked improvement after April, he needs better command of his stuff. He spent most of his time in the AFL trying to hone his changeup. Kimbrel has moved quicker than expected and is Atlanta's closer of the future. More time in Triple-A wold benefit him, but he could make his major league debut in the second half of 2010.

— **By Bill Ballew**

MINOR LEAGUE MENTIONS BY BA

YEAR	TOP 100	ORG RANKING	LEAGUE RANKING	BEST TOOLS
2008			**No. 14:** Appalachian	
2009		**No. 10:** Braves		**CAR:** Best Fastball
2010		**No. 5:** Braves		
2011	No. 86	**No. 5:** Braves		

COREY KLUBER, RHP

BIOGRAPHY

PROPER NAME: Corey Scott Kluber. **BORN:** April 10, 1986 in Birmingham, Ala.
HT: 6-4. **WT:** 215. **BATS:** R. **THROWS:** R. **SCHOOL:** Stetson.
FIRST PRO CONTRACT: Selected by Padres in fourth round (134th overall) of 2007 draft;
signed July 17, 2007.

CLEVELAND INDIANS TOP 30 PROSPECTS FOR 2011

The Indians, Cardinals and Padres pulled off a three-way deal at the July 31 trade deadline, with Cleveland sending Jake Westbrook to St. Louis and getting Kluber from San Diego in return. He led the Double-A Texas League with 136 strikeouts despite leaving the circuit after the trade.

He racks up whiffs more with his deceptive short-arm delivery than with pure stuff. Kluber does have a solid arsenal of pitches, working mainly off his 88-92 mph fastball and average slider. He also flashes an average changeup and throws strikes.

He still needs to refine his command, because he's around the strike zone almost too much and is fairly hittable. He'd durable, having made 82 starts and worked 455 innings in his three full pro seasons.

Kluber doesn't have high upside, but he has good feel for pitching and could be a back-of-the-rotation starter. He'll open 2011 in the Columbus rotation after finishing last season with two starts there.

— **By Ben Badler**

MINOR LEAGUE MENTIONS BY BA

YEAR	TOP 100	ORG RANKING	LEAGUE RANKING	BEST TOOLS
2008		**No. 29:** Padres		
2009				
2010				
2011		**No. 26:** Indians		
2012			**No. 12:** International	**IL:** Best Breaking Pitch

BARRY LARKIN, SS

BIOGRAPHY

PROPER NAME: Barry Louis Larkin. **BORN:** April 28, 1964 in Cincinnati.
HT: 6-0. **WT:** 185. **BATS:** R. **THROWS:** R. **SCHOOL:** Michigan.
FIRST PRO CONTRACT: Selected by Reds in first round (fourth overall) of 1985 draft;
signed June 3, 1985.

TOP COLLEGE PROSPECTS FOR 1985 DRAFT

A former football standout at Cincinnati's famed Moeller High School, Larkin has elected to pursue baseball only at Michigan. While scouts are in general agreement that he's the best shortstop prospect in the country, he's not mechanically sound yet — largely because of his Northern background.

"He hasn't regressed at all since high school," said one scouting director, "and with a lack of infielders in the draft this year, you might see some over-drafting at shortstop, which wouldn't hurt Larkin."

— **By Allan Simpson**

CINCINNATI REDS TOP 10 PROSPECTS FOR 1986

When Larkin came out of Cincinnati's Moeller High School in 1982, the Reds thought enough of him to make him a second-round selection. Larkin, however, turned them down and decided to go to the University of Michigan.

The Reds never gave up hope, and when Larkin was eligible in the draft again last summer, they used their No. 1 pick to take him. This time he signed, and he gave the Reds nothing but reason for optimism with his debut.

Larkin looked right at home in AA, hitting .267 for Vermont. He didn't show power (one home run in 255 at-bats), but that will come. They key for him was just getting his feet on the ground, and he was not overpowered by the high level of competition. He will have good power for a shortstop. In fact, he should hit enough that he could be moved to third base.

It would only be because of Stillwell that Larkin would have to change positions. He's got the range and natural actions of a shortstop, and good enough arm strength to play the position on turf.

— **By Tracy Ringolsby**

MINOR LEAGUE MENTIONS BY BA

YEAR	TOP 100	ORG RANKING	LEAGUE RANKING	BEST TOOLS
1986		**No. 8:** Reds		**AA:** Best Defensive SS

CLIFF LEE, LHP

BIOGRAPHY

PROPER NAME: Clifton Phifer Lee. **BORN:** August 30, 1978 in Benton, Ark.
HT: 6-3. **WT:** 205. **BATS:** L. **THROWS:** L. **SCHOOL:** Benton (Ark.) HS.
FIRST PRO CONTRACT: Selected by Montreal Expos in fourth round (105th overall) of 2000 draft; signed July 6, 2000.

CLEVELAND INDIANS TOP 10 PROSPECTS FOR 2003

After coming to the Indians in the Bartolo Colon deal, Lee jumped from Double-A to Triple-A to the big leagues, getting rave reviews at each level. Lee is a rare pitcher who can win without his best stuff. And when he's on, watch out.

His fastball sits at 91-93 mph, his slider has good late action, and his curveball and changeup give hitters something else to worry about. Lee is so smooth that hitters don't get a good read on his pitches until they're halfway to the plate. Lee's velocity was down to the high 80s in September, probably because his innings jumped in 2002. He just needs to adjust to the majors and appreciate the importance of every pitch.

Lee is a candidate to win one of the openings in the rotation behind C.C. Sabathia. He, Billy Traber and Brian Tallet give Cleveland three advanced southpaws, and Lee has the most upside.

— **By Jim Ingraham**

MINOR LEAGUE MENTIONS BY BA

YEAR	TOP 100	ORG RANKING	LEAGUE RANKING	BEST TOOLS
2001		No. 21: Expos		
2002		No. 11: Expos	No. 5: Eastern	EL: Best Breaking Pitch
2003	No. 30	No. 3: Indians	No. 8: International	

JON LESTER, LHP

BIOGRAPHY

PROPER NAME: Jonathan Tyler Lester. **BORN:** January 7, 1984 in Tacoma.
HT: 6-4. **WT:** 240. **BATS:** L. **THROWS:** L. **SCHOOL:** Bellarmine Prep, Tacoma.
FIRST PRO CONTRACT: Selected by Red Sox in second round (57th overall) of 2002 draft;
signed Aug. 13, 2002.

BOSTON RED SOX TOP 10 PROSPECTS FOR 2005

Lester gets asked about in trade talks more than any Red Sox prospect, and he would have gone to the Rangers had Boston been able to finalize a deal for Alex Rodriguez last offseason. The top pick in the Red Sox' last draft before they adopted a strong college emphasis, he signed for $1 million as a second-rounder.

Lester has a stronger arm than most lefthanders, as he pitches at 92-93 mph and hits 96. He's very athletic and has a smooth delivery, which bodes well for his long-term control. He does an excellent job of keeping the ball down in the zone, yielding just nine homers in 197 pro innings. He picked up an effective cut fastball at midseason. He's far from a finished product. Lester's curveball and changeup have the potential to be average or better pitches, but they're not there yet. He missed most of June with shoulder tightness, but it's not a long-term concern.

How well Lester refines his secondary pitches will determine when he reaches Boston and where he'll slot into the rotation. He'll open 2005 in Double-A and could surface in the majors as early as mid-2006.

— **By Jim Callis**

MINOR LEAGUE MENTIONS BY BA

YEAR	TOP 100	ORG RANKING	LEAGUE RANKING	BEST TOOLS
2003		**No. 8:** Red Sox		
2004		**No. 8:** Red Sox	**No. 15:** Florida State	
2005		**No. 4:** Red Sox	**No. 4:** Eastern	
2006	No. 22	**No. 2:** Red Sox		

TIM LINCECUM, RHP

BIOGRAPHY

PROPER NAME: Timothy LeRoy Lincecum. **BORN:** June 15, 1984 in Bellevue, Wash.
HT: 5-11. **WT:** 170. **BATS:** L. **THROWS:** R. **SCHOOL:** Washington.
FIRST PRO CONTRACT: Selected by Giants in first round (10th overall) of 2006 draft; signed June 30, 2006.

SAN FRANCISCO GIANTS TOP 10 PROSPECTS FOR 2007

When Lincecum was available with the 10th overall pick in the 2006 draft, the Giants felt like they had just won the lottery. After a couple of tuneups with short-season Salem Keizer, Lincecum dominated at high Class A San Jose and struck out 10 over seven innings to win his lone playoff start.

Lincecum throws a 91-96 mph fastball that tops out at 98. If that weren't enough, he also has a true hammer curveball that breaks early and keeps on breaking. Giants scouts believe he might have the best curve of any drafted player since Kerry Wood. He added a changeup during his Cape (Cod) stint, and at times it's a swing-and-miss pitch that bottoms out at the plate. During the spring, he also unveiled a hard slider that he can throw for strikes. Lincecum's combination of stuff and deception makes him close to unhittable. He's incredibly strong for a pitcher his size, and some old-timers say he reminds them of Bob Feller or a righthanded Sandy Koufax because of his delivery and flexibility. That's no coincidence, because Lincecum's father watched Koufax pitch and taught his son to copy the Hall of Famer's mechanics.

Lincecum logged 342 innings in his three seasons at Washington, frequently exceeding 120 pitches per start. While he claims to have never felt soreness in his arm, some scouts believe he's a breakdown waiting to happen. He could be the devastating closer the Giants have lacked since Robb Nen injured his shoulder in 2002, but they say Lincecum will be a starter until he proves he can't handle the role. If he dominates, San Francisco will have a hard time keeping him off the Opening Day roster.

— **By Andy Baggarly**

MINOR LEAGUE MENTIONS BY BA

YEAR	TOP 100	ORG RANKING	LEAGUE RANKING	BEST TOOLS
2007	No. 11	**No. 1:** Giants		**PCL:** Best Pitching Prospect, Best Fastball, Best Breaking Pitch

FRANCISCO LINDOR, SS

BIOGRAPHY

PROPER NAME: Francisco Miguel Lindor. **BORN:** November 14, 1993 in Caguas, Puerto Rico.
HT: 5-11. **WT:** 190. **BATS:** B. **THROWS:** R. **SCHOOL:** Montverde (Fla.) Academy.
FIRST PRO CONTRACT: Selected by Indians in first round (eighth overall) of 2011 draft;
signed August 15, 2011.

CLEVELAND INDIANS TOP 10 PROSPECTS FOR 2013

Known for typically college-heavy drafts, the Indians drafted Lindor with the eighth overall pick in 2011, making him their first prep first-rounder since Dan Denham and Alan Horne in 2001. Lindor signed for $2.9 million, the biggest bonus Cleveland ever has given a position player or high school draftee.

An excellent athlete, Lindor is one of the best defensive shortstops in the minors. In addition to above-average defensive tools, he has phenomenal instincts. He knows how to position himself and always seems to be in the right spot at the right time. He gets great reads off the bat and has terrific fundamentals. His range and arm are both better than average. Lindor has a quiet, simple approach in the batter's box. He has a compact swing with good bat speed from both sides of the plate and hits line drives to all fields. His pitch-recognition skills are above average. Lindor could be a plus hitter who gets on base at a high clip, though his power is more to the gaps than over the fence. He's a slightly above-average runner whose 27 steals in 2012 were somewhat of a surprise, though he needs to become more efficient after getting thrown out 12 times.

Lindor has the look of a future all-star shortstop. Ticketed for high Class A Carolina in 2013, he's the best infield prospect the franchise has had since Brandon Phillips and the best position prospect who was originally signed by the Indians since Victor Martinez.

— **By Ben Badler**

MINOR LEAGUE MENTIONS BY BA

YEAR	TOP 100	ORG RANKING	LEAGUE RANKING	BEST TOOLS
2012	No. 37	**No. 1:** Indians	**No. 3:** Midwest	**MWL:** Best Defensive SS
2013	No. 28	**No. 1:** Indians	**No. 1:** Carolina	**CAR:** Best Defensive SS, Most Exciting Player
2014	No. 13	**No. 1:** Indians	**No. 3:** Eastern **No. 3:** International	**EL:** Best Defensive SS, Best INF Arm
2015	No. 19	**No. 1:** Indians	**No. 1:** International	**IL:** Best Defensive SS, Most Exciting Player

KENNY LOFTON, OF

BIOGRAPHY

PROPER NAME: Kenneth Lofton. **BORN:** May 31, 1967 in East Chicago, Ind.
HT: 6-0. **WT:** 180. **BATS:** L. **THROWS:** L. **SCHOOL:** Arizona.
FIRST PRO CONTRACT: Selected by Astros in 17th round (428th overall) of 1988 draft; signed June 16, 1988.

CLEVELAND INDIANS TOP 10 PROSPECTS FOR 1992

Acquired from Houston at the Winter Meetings, Lofton immediately bolted to the head of the class. He didn't come cheap: Lost was Eddie Taubensee, a lefthanded hitting catcher who probably would be among the top five prospects on this list were he still in the organization.

Lofton is faster, much better defensively, a better bunter and younger than Alex Cole.

"We kept reading through our reports and asking people about him, and we couldn't find anyone who would say anything negative," Indians manager Mike Hargrove said.

A prototype leadoff hitter and center fielder, Lofton will get ample opportunity to unseat Cole in spring training. With 168 stolen bases in four professional seasons, Lofton knows how to run. But he also knows how to get caught: his 55 percent success rate is unbecoming of one so swift.

There is also a contact question. In the minor leagues Lofton has struck out once every 5.3 at bats, a distressing figure for a leadoff hitter.

But given their casual approach to the present, Indians officials can live with Lofton's growing pains.

— **By Jim Ingraham**

MINOR LEAGUE MENTIONS BY BA

YEAR	TOP 100	ORG RANKING	LEAGUE RANKING	BEST TOOLS
1991	No. 75	**No. 4:** Astros	**No. 1:** Pacific Coast	**PCL:** Best Baserunner, Fastest Baserunner, Most Exciting Player
1992	No. 28	**No. 1:** Indians		

EVAN LONGORIA, 3B

BIOGRAPHY

PROPER NAME: Evan Michael Longoria. **BORN:** October 7, 1985 in Downey, Calif.
HT: 6-1. **WT:** 215. **BATS:** R. **THROWS:** R. **SCHOOL:** Long Beach State.
FIRST PRO CONTRACT: Selected by Rays in first round (third overall) of 2006 draft;
signed June 7, 2006.

TAMPA BAY RAYS TOP 10 PROSPECTS FOR 2007

The Devil Rays planned on taking a pitcher with the third overall pick in the June draft, but changed their plans when Longoria unexpectedly fell to them. The 2005 Cape Cod League MVP signed for $3 million on draft day after batting .353/.468/.602 as a junior at Long Beach State.

Known for his bat, he hit even more than expected in his pro debut, whacking 21 homers (counting the playoffs) and reaching Double-A Montgomery. Longoria had no problem adjusting to wood bats in pro ball. His quick hands generate plenty of bat speed, allowing him to hit for average and power. He projects as a .300 hitter with 30 or more homers annually. He played some shortstop in college and shows soft hands and a solid arm at third base. His competitiveness and makeup are considered major pluses.

Longoria has no glaring shortcomings. He just needs to be more consistent in all phases of his game, something that should come easily with experience. His worst tool is his speed but even that is average.

Easily the most advanced hitter in the 2006 draft, Longoria may reach Tampa Bay sooner than initially expected. He could push for a big league job in mid-2007 and has the talent to become an all-star at third base.

— **By Bill Ballew**

MINOR LEAGUE MENTIONS BY BA

YEAR	TOP 100	ORG RANKING	LEAGUE RANKING	BEST TOOLS
2007	No. 7	**No. 2:** Rays	**No. 2:** Southern	**SL:** Best Power
2008	No. 2	**No. 1:** Rays		

MANNY MACHADO, 3B

BIOGRAPHY

PROPER NAME: Manuel Arturo Machado. **BORN:** July 6, 1992 in Hialeah, Fla.
HT: 6-3. **WT:** 185. **BATS:** R. **THROWS:** R. **SCHOOL:** Brito Miami Private HS.
FIRST PRO CONTRACT: Selected by Orioles in first round (third overall) of 2010 draft;
signed August 16, 2010.

BALTIMORE ORIOLES TOP 10 PROSPECTS FOR 2012

The scouting consensus was that the top three players in the 2010 draft--Bryce Harper, Jameson Taillon and Machado—were a cut above everyone else, so the Orioles were happy to grab their shortstop of the future with the No. 3 overall choice after the Nationals picked Harper and Pirates selected Taillon.

The Orioles brought in J.J. Hardy to fill their gaping hole at shortstop, but long-term they had no one in the system to take over the position until signing Machado, who has legitimate five-tool ability. He has a good swing and bat speed. He makes consistent hard contact—he struck out just three times in 36 pro at-bats—and repeatedly puts the barrel on the ball. The ball already carries well off his bat, and he has the room to add muscle to his wiry 6-foot-3 frame. Baltimore believes he can become a .300 hitter with 20 homers a season as he matures. Machado also has the arm, build and strength to be a major league shortstop. He shows advanced defensive skills, with solid range, soft hands and a plus arm. His weakest tool is his speed, but even that rates as fringe average.

Machado has all the tools and just needs to play. Because of his build, Dominican bloodlines and hype as a shortstop coming out of South Florida, he earns obvious Alex Rodriguez comparisons. He's not as physically mature as Rodriguez was when he came into pro ball, and his ceiling isn't as lofty, but Machado still has the look of a perennial all-star. He'll open his first full season at low Class A Delmarva, and should move quickly through the system if he hits as expected. He could be ready for Baltimore at some point in 2013.

— By Will Lingo

MINOR LEAGUE MENTIONS BY BA

YEAR	TOP 100	ORG RANKING	LEAGUE RANKING	BEST TOOLS
2011	No. 14	**No. 1:** Orioles	**No. 2:** South Atlantic **No. 1:** Eastern	
2012	No. 11	**No. 2:** Orioles	**No. 1:** Eastern	**EL:** Best Defensive SS, Best INF Arm, Most Exciting Player

GREG MADDUX, RHP

BIOGRAPHY

PROPER NAME: Gregory Alan Maddux. **BORN:** April 14, 1966 in San Angelo, Texas.
HT: 6-0. **WT:** 195. **BATS:** R. **THROWS:** R. **SCHOOL:** Valley HS, Las Vegas.
FIRST PRO CONTRACT: Selected by Cubs in second round of 1984 draft; signed June 19, 1984.

APPALACHIAN LEAGUE TOP 10 PROSPECTS FOR 1984

Drafted in the second round in June by the Chicago Cubs, Maddux impressed managers with an overpowering fastball, despite a slight build.

"He's got a live arm," said (Bluefield manager Greg) Biagini. "It's loose and limber, and he knows how to pitch ... He throws hard for his size."

"He's the best pitcher in the league." said (Pikeville manager Jim) Fairey. "He throws 90, he's young (18), he has a good curve. And he has poise."

Maddux, whose older brother Mike is a pitcher in the Phillies system, was 6-2 in his first pro season, with a 2.63 ERA. He struck out 62 in 86 innings.

— By Allan Simpson

CHICAGO CUBS TOP 10 PROSPECTS FOR 1987

He is the most advanced pitcher in the system and would be their best prospect if he was 20 pounds stronger. Maddux rushed through Pittsfield and Iowa last season (14-4, 2.91, with 45 walks and 100 strikeouts in 192 innings), but was hit hard in a September trial with the Cubs.

He has a good fastball that he can run inside or cut away, but it will be a five-inning pitch if he doesn't get stronger. His changeup is above average and his curve is strong when he pulls down properly. But in his immediate favor, he is not afraid to pitch inside and his control is superb, which could land him on the varsity this year as a spot starter and long reliever.

— By Ken Leiker

MINOR LEAGUE MENTIONS BY BA

YEAR	TOP 100	ORG RANKING	LEAGUE RANKING	BEST TOOLS
1984			**No. 4:** Appalachian	
1985		**No. 5:** Cubs		
1986		**No. 7:** Cubs		
1987		**No. 5:** Cubs		

BaseBall
america

SIMPLY
THE BEST
GREG MADDUX MASTERS
THE ART OF PITCHING

COMPLETE AMATEUR
DRAFT LIST

OKLAHOMA WINS THE
COLLEGE WORLD SERIES

FRESHMAN OF THE YEAR:
TENNESSEE'S R.A. DICKEY

MAJOR LEAGUE
ORGANIZATION
REPORTS

ESPN'S PETER
GAMMONS

MINOR LEAGUE STAT KINGS
BERNARDO BRITO, NICK CAPRA

RUSSELL MARTIN, C

BIOGRAPHY

PROPER NAME: Russell Nathan Coltrane Martin.
BORN: February 15, 1983 in East York, Canada.
HT: 5-10. **WT:** 205. **BATS:** R. **THROWS:** R. **SCHOOL:** Chipola (Fla.) JC.
FIRST PRO CONTRACT: Selected by Dodgers in 17th round (511th overall) of 2002 draft; signed June 13, 2002.

LOS ANGELES DODGERS TOP 10 PROSPECTS FOR 2006

Area scout Clarence Johns (now with the Rockies) scouted Martin as a third baseman and immediately projected him to catch. Martin has become one of the best catching prospects in the game, thanks to his athleticism and ability to absorb instruction.

Martin employs a patient approach at the plate and uses the entire field. His swing is compact and simple, he stays through the ball well and he's a good situational hitter. He's comfortable behind the plate and his blocking and receiving skills are advanced for such an inexperienced catcher. He has a strong, accurate arm, good footwork and an efficient exchange on throws. Martin has yet to show much power, though he can drive balls out of the park when he stays back. Some scouts believe he'll be a 15-20 homer threat in time. He has slightly below-average speed, but he's fast for a catcher and isn't afraid to take an extra base.

Martin is similar to former Dodgers catcher Paul LoDuca, with better defensive skills and slightly less offensive ability. He'll probably begin 2006 in Triple-A but could reach Los Angeles in the second half.

— **By Alan Matthews**

MINOR LEAGUE MENTIONS BY BA

YEAR	TOP 100	ORG RANKING	LEAGUE RANKING	BEST TOOLS
2004		**No. 18:** Dodgers		
2005	No. 89	**No. 6:** Dodgers	**No. 10:** Southern	**SL:** Best Strike-Zone Judgment, Best Defensive C
2006	No. 42	**No. 4:** Dodgers		

EDGAR MARTINEZ, DH

BIOGRAPHY

PROPER NAME: Edgar Martinez. **BORN:** January 2, 1963 in New York, N.Y.
HT: 5-11. **WT:** 210. **BATS:** R. **THROWS:** R. **SCHOOL:** American College, Puerto Rico.
FIRST PRO CONTRACT: Signed as international free agent by Mariners, Dec. 19, 1982.

SEATTLE MARINERS TOP 10 PROSPECTS FOR 1985

What a difference a year made for Martinez. After being signed out of Puerto Rico in 1982, he debuted at Bellingham and there was little hope for his development. He hit a weak .173. During the offseason, however, he matured physically and came back last summer much stronger.

The 300-foot fly ball outs suddenly went 350 feet, and the ground balls in the hole went through the hole. He drove the ball and hit for average at Wausau (.303, 32 doubles, 15 HRs, 66 RBIs). If he continues to develop with the bat, he can play third base. He has average speed, good reactions and a good arm.

SEATTLE MARINERS TOP 10 PROSPECTS FOR 1988

He's the cousin of San Diego's power-hitting Carmelo Martinez, but other than the ancestry has little in common with Carmelo. Edgar, signed as a free agent out of Puerto Rico in December 1982, is a disciplined hitter. Consider: a .294 average and 340 walks compared to 181 strikeouts in the last four pro seasons.

He works himself ahead in the count, and makes use of all fields, driving the ball into the alleys. While he'll never be a big home run hitter — maybe 15 to 20 a year — Martinez's discipline will produce runs. He's averaged 70 RBIs the last four years. In the field, he's solid, with good reactions and the soft hands of a middle infielder.

— By Tracy Ringolsby

MINOR LEAGUE MENTIONS BY BA

YEAR	TOP 100	ORG RANKING	LEAGUE RANKING	BEST TOOLS
1985		**No. 7:** Mariners		
1986				**SL:** Best Defensive 3B
1987				
1988		**No. 6:** Mariners		
1989		**No. 3:** Mariners		

PEDRO MARTINEZ, RHP

BIOGRAPHY

PROPER NAME: Pedro Jaime Martinez.
BORN: October 25, 1971 in Manoguayabo, Dominican Republic.
HT: 5-11. **WT:** 195. **BATS:** R. **THROWS:** R.
FIRST PRO CONTRACT: Signed as international free agent by Dodgers, June 18, 1988.

LOS ANGELES DODGERS TOP 10 PROSPECTS FOR 1992

All you need to know about Pedro Martínez is that the Dodgers think he could be better than his brother Ramon, who has 44 major league wins before his 24th birthday.

Even an organization known to advance players exceedingly slowly couldn't hold back Pedro, who raced from Class A Bakersfield to finish last year at Triple-A Albuquerque, succeeding at each level.

Martínez was a combined 18-8, 2.29. He does not throw as hard as Ramon and is on the short side for a righthander, but Pedro is years ahead of his lanky older brother with the curveball, and he makes up for his lack of experience with exceptional intelligence. He digests instruction, and is capable of exploiting a batter's weakness to a degree rarely seen in a 20-year-old.

His 184 strikeouts in 1991 are the most for a Dodgers minor leaguer since Sid Fernandez had 209 in 1983. His 18 wins were the most since Ted Power had 20 in 1981.

Martínez spent September with his brother in Los Angeles, and heard constant comparisons. "That pressure is not fair," he said. "People look at me like I'm a big, big man. Compare me to a big league all-star? I'm not Ramon. People who know about baseball won't do that."

— By Ken Gurnick

MINOR LEAGUE MENTIONS BY BA

YEAR	TOP 100	ORG RANKING	LEAGUE RANKING	BEST TOOLS
1990			**No. 3:** Pioneer	
1991		**No. 8:** Dodgers	**No. 1:** California **No. 5:** Texas	**CAL:** Best Pitching Prospect, Best Fastball **TL:** Best Pitching Prospect
1992	No. 10	**No. 1:** Dodgers	**No. 3:** Pacific Coast	**PCL:** Best Fastball
1993	No. 62	**No. 5:** Dodgers		

DON MATTINGLY, 1B

BIOGRAPHY

PROPER NAME: Donald Arthur Mattingly. **BORN:** April 20, 1961 in Evansville, Ind.
HT: 6-0. **WT:** 175. **BATS:** L. **THROWS:** L. **SCHOOL:** Reitz Memorial HS, Evansville, Ind.
FIRST PRO CONTRACT: Selected by Yankees in 19th round (493rd overall) of 1979 draft;
signed June 5, 1979.

NEW YORK YANKEES TOP 10 PROSPECTS FOR 1983

Mattingly has hit .331 in his four pro seasons and struck out only 118 times in 1,683 official at bats. He's advanced a level each year, averaging nine homers and 93 RBIs the last three seasons, and he finished last September with the Yankees.

Mattingly, 22 in April, hits lefthanded and fields adequately. But he has little power and no speed, either of which would place him in much higher regard.

— **By Ken Leiker**

AMERICAN LEAGUE ROOKIE PREVIEW; 1983

Twenty-one-year-old Don Mattingly (.315, 10 HRs, 75 RBIs) shows promise. He has excellent bat speed and could develop legitimate power, a must for a lefthanded hitter in Yankee Stadium. Solid defensive outfielder.

— **By Tracy Ringolsby**

MINOR LEAGUE MENTIONS BY BA

YEAR	TOP 100	ORG RANKING	LEAGUE RANKING	BEST TOOLS
1983		No. 9: Yankees		

JOE MAUER, C

BIOGRAPHY

PROPER NAME: Joseph Patrick Mauer. **BORN:** April 19, 1983 in St. Paul, mINN.
HT: 6-5. **WT:** 225. **BATS:** L. **THROWS:** R. **SCHOOL:** Cretin-Derham Hall HS, St. Paul, Minn.
FIRST PRO CONTRACT: Selected by Twins in first round (first overall) of 2001 draft;
signed July 17, 2001.

MINNESOTA TWINS TOP 10 PROSPECTS FOR 2003

Holding the No. 1 pick in the 2001 draft, the Twins opted for Baseball America High School Player of the Year Joe Mauer instead of consensus top talent Mark Prior, who was out of their price range. The Twins signed Mauer to a franchise-record $5.15 million deal, and he started his pro career by hitting .400 for Rookie-level Elizabethon. He raked for low Class A Quad City in his first full season, which ended early thanks to double-hernia surgery.

Mauer shows outstanding balance at the plate and generates outstanding bat speed with a smooth, classic lefthanded stroke. A natural hitter, he covers the plate well, understands the strike zone and makes consistent, hard contact to all fields. He has a knack for finding the sweet spot when he connects with the ball. The ball carries well off his bat, and he'll develop above-average power as he continues to bulk up his loose, athletic frame and learns which pitches to turn on. He already shows plus power in batting practice. Mauer's arm is near the top of the scale, but more important, he's mechanically sound with a quick release and his throws are right on the bag.

Mauer needs to learn the nuances of the game, including working with pitchers during a game. With his makeup and feel, he'll be a complete receiver. More at-bats will help him understand counts and when to attack pitches. Mauer is primed for a speedy ascent. A.J. Pierzynski's emergence will help the Twins bide their time, though it will be tempting to promote him aggressively. He'll own the top spot on this list until he takes over in Minnesota.

— **By Josh Boyd**

MINOR LEAGUE MENTIONS BY BA

YEAR	TOP 100	ORG RANKING	LEAGUE RANKING	BEST TOOLS
2001			**No. 1:** Appalachian	
2002	No. 7	**No. 1:** Twins	**No. 1:** Midwest	**MWL:** Best Defensive C
2003	No. 4	**No. 1:** Twins	**No. 1:** Florida State	**FSL:** Best Hitter, Best Defensive C
2004	No. 1	**No. 1:** Twins	**No. 1:** Eastern	
2005	No. 1	**No. 1:** Twins		

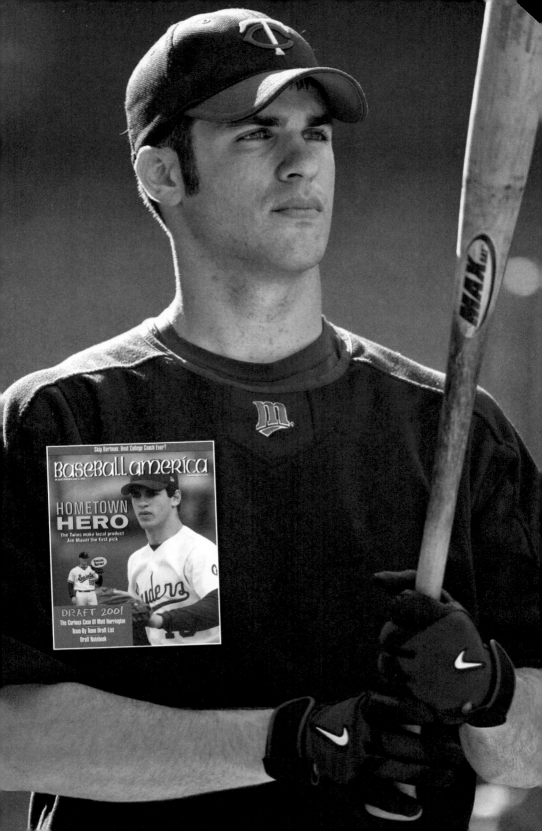

BRIAN McCANN, C

BIOGRAPHY

PROPER NAME: Brian Michael McCann. **BORN:** February 20, 1984 in Athens, Ga.
HT: 6-3. **WT:** 225. **BATS:** L. **THROWS:** R. **SCHOOL:** Duluth (Ga.) HS.
FIRST PRO CONTRACT: Drafted by Braves in second round (64th overall) of 2002 draft;
signed June 11, 2002.

ATLANTA BRAVES TOP 10 PROSPECTS FOR 2005

Despite playing at pitcher-friendly Myrtle Beach, McCann put together one of the best all-around seasons of any catcher in the minors. A Carolina League all-star, he tied for the organization lead in doubles and set a career high for homers. Older brother Brad, a third baseman, signed with the Marlins as a 2004 sixth-round pick, and his father Howard is the former head coach at Marshall.

McCann has a sweet lefthanded swing and as much raw power as anyone in the organization. He employs a disciplined approach at the plate and makes solid contact. Drafted primarily for his bat, he has dedicated himself to improving behind the plate and was named the CL's best defensive catcher. He threw out 30 percent of basestealers with his strong, accurate arm and quick release. While pitchers like throwing to McCann, he needs to hone his skills behind the plate, particularly his footwork and agility. Offensively, he could draw more walks. He's a below-average runner.

He has drawn comparisons to Eddie Taubensee, but the Braves say McCann has a higher ceiling. He'll spend 2005 at the new Double-A Mississippi affiliate and could reach Atlanta by late 2006.

— By Bill Ballew

MINOR LEAGUE MENTIONS BY BA

YEAR	TOP 100	ORG RANKING	LEAGUE RANKING	BEST TOOLS
2002			**No. 20:** Gulf Coast	
2003		**No. 28:** Braves	**No. 20:** South Atlantic	
2004		**No. 7:** Braves	**No. 8:** Carolina	**CAR:** Best Defensive C
2005	No. 44	**No. 3:** Braves	**No. 9:** Southern	

ANDREW McCUTCHEN, OF

BIOGRAPHY

PROPER NAME: Andrew Stefan McCutchen. **BORN:** October 10, 1986 in Fort Meade, Fla.
HT: 5-11. **WT:** 195. **BATS:** R. **THROWS:** R. **SCHOOL:** Fort Meade (Fla.) HS.
FIRST PRO CONTRACT: Selected by Pirates in first round (11th overall) of 2005 draft;
signed June 16, 2005.

PITTSBURGH PIRATES TOP 10 PROSPECTS FOR 2009

McCutchen ranked No. 1 on this list the past two years, as well as in the Rookie-level Gulf Coast League in 2005 and the low Class A South Atlantic League in 2006. He reached Double-A as a teenager and rated as the No. 2 prospect in the Triple-A International League, where managers tabbed him as the league's most exciting player.

McCutchen has quick hands and recognizes pitches extremely well, giving him the ability to wait for the ball to get deeper in the zone while drawing his share of walks. He has outstanding speed that makes him a basestealing threat and a potential Gold Glover. He has outstanding instincts and an average arm in center field.

McCutchen is susceptible to breaking pitches, in part because he gets pull-happy, and his power hasn't developed as hoped. He's slow getting out of the batter's box, which prevents him from getting as many infield hits as his speed suggests he should. He still has work to do as a basestealer after leading all Triple-A players by getting caught 19 times in 2008.

Though he's the Pirates' center fielder of the near future, McCutchen is slated to return to Indianapolis to start the season. He once looked like a No. 3 hitter but now profiles as a leadoff man.

— **By John Perrotto**

MINOR LEAGUE MENTIONS BY BA

YEAR	TOP 100	ORG RANKING	LEAGUE RANKING	BEST TOOLS
2005			**No. 1:** Gulf Coast	
2006	No. 50	**No. 2:** Pirates	**No. 1:** South Atlantic	
2007	No. 13	**No. 1:** Pirates	**No. 2:** Eastern	**EL:** Most Exciting Player
2008	No. 13	**No. 1:** Pirates	**No. 2:** International	**IL:** Most Exciting Player
2009	No. 33	**No. 2:** Pirates	**No. 3:** International	**IL:** Fastest Baserunner, Most Exciting Player

JACK McDOWELL, RHP

BIOGRAPHY

PROPER NAME: Jack Burns McDowell. **BORN:** January 16, 1966 in Van Nuys, Calif.
HT: 6-5. **WT:** 180. **BATS:** R. **THROWS:** R. **SCHOOL:** Stanford.
FIRST PRO CONTRACT: Selected by the White Sox in first round (fifth overall) of 1987 draft;
signed July 29, 1987.

TOP 25 HIGH SCHOOL PROSPECTS FOR 1984 MLB DRAFT

The outstanding prospect in the fertile San Fernando Valley area north of Los Angeles, scouts particularly like McDowell's size (6-5, 180) and makeup (he's already signed with Stanford). Through his first 38 innings this season, McDowell was 5-0 with a 0.37 ERA and had struck out 45 while walking 14. A year ago, he was 7-1 with a 0.85 ERA for Notre Dame. According to McDowell, his best pitch is his fastball, but he uses a forkball for his strikeout pitch. McDowell plays shortstop when not pitching, and through 14 games was hitting .512 with three homers and 19 RBIs.

CHICAGO WHITE SOX TOP 10 PROSPECTS FOR 1988

The fifth player selected last June, McDowell could be the Opening Day starter and is an early favorite for Rookie of the Year.

McDowell was brilliant in four starts for the Sox last September (3-0, 1.93 ERA), after a rough breaking-in period at Sarasota and Birmingham (1-3, 6.51). His problems disappeared after the Sox tightened his delivery, which stabilized his release point.

McDowell's fastball is consistent at 87-89 mph and has been clocked as high as 93 mph. His forkball and slider are power pitches but need to become more consistent. The Sox rave about his maturity and presence on the mound, which is a trait that all pitchers seem to carry out of Stanford.

— **By Ken Leiker**

MINOR LEAGUE MENTIONS BY BA

YEAR	TOP 100	ORG RANKING	LEAGUE RANKING	BEST TOOLS
1988		**No. 1:** White Sox		

FRED McGRIFF, 1B

BIOGRAPHY

PROPER NAME: Frederick Stanley McGriff. **BORN:** October 31, 1963 in Tampa.
HT: 6-3. **WT:** 215. **BATS:** L. **THROWS:** L. **SCHOOL:** Jefferson HS, Tampa.
FIRST PRO CONTRACT: Selected by Yankees in ninth round (233rd overall) of 1981 draft;
signed June 11, 1981.

TORONTO BLUE JAYS TOP 10 PROSPECTS FOR 1984

What the Blue Jays scouting system hasn't uncovered at the Amateur level, it has found awaiting in the New York Yankee farm system. The Jays acquired McGriff a year ago as part of the package for Dale Murray. It will still be some time before he makes the Yankees regret that deal more than ever, but the time should come.

McGriff is the legitimate power hitter — the type, who with the inviting elements for a lefthanded hitter in Toronto, could be capable of 30 to 40 home runs. In his first full professional season last summer, he hit 28 home runs and drove in 93 runs, splitting the time between Kinston and Florence.

Like most young men with power, he creates some big breezes, too (147 strikeouts, 469 at-bats). That will decrease as his experience and knowledge of the strike zone increases, but it's foolish to think he'll be a pure contact hitter.

He does not have a great deal of lateral movement, but then he is a first baseman. But he has soft hands, and an excellent arm. He will field anything he gets, too, even if that's not as much as some would like.

He needs to increase his reaction time and get experience, but with his makeup and power it won't be long before he makes the step to the big leagues.

— **By Tracy Ringolsby**

MINOR LEAGUE MENTIONS BY BA

YEAR	TOP 100	ORG RANKING	LEAGUE RANKING	BEST TOOLS
1983		**No. 5:** Blue Jays	**No. 5:** Carolina	
1984		**No. 2:** Blue Jays		
1985		**No. 1:** Blue Jays		
1986		**No. 7:** Blue Jays		

MARK McGWIRE, 1B

BIOGRAPHY

PROPER NAME: Mark David McGwire. **BORN:** October 1, 1963 in Pomona, Calif.
HT: 6-5. **WT:** 225. **BATS:** R. **THROWS:** R. **SCHOOL:** Southern California.l
FIRST PRO CONTRACT: Selected by the Athletics in the first round (10th overall) of the 1984
draft; signed July 20, 1984.

OAKLAND ATHLETICS TOP 10 PROSPECTS FOR 1985

The best power-hitting prospect in the college ranks last season, his stats at Southern Cal and on the Olympic team totaled a .378 average, 38 HRs and 106 RBIs. McGwire was burned out mentally and bothered by a sore hamstring by the time he reported to the California League (.200, 1 HR and 21 strikeouts in 55 at-bats), but did pull himself together for the playoffs (8-for-15).

A first baseman in college, McGwire was moved to third during the instructional league. He's awfully big for the position, but the A's think his body is supple enough to play there. There's no question about his arm (he was an outstanding pitching prospect his freshman year at USC), and the A's say he has shown quick hands.

Once he learns not to commit himself too early at the plate, scouts think McGwire will take off offensively. As a hitter, he's ready for Double-A, but because of the move to third, he probably will start this season in the California League.

— **By Ken Leiker**

MINOR LEAGUE MENTIONS BY BA

YEAR	TOP 100	ORG RANKING	LEAGUE RANKING	BEST TOOLS
1985		**No. 5:** Athletics		
1986		**No. 6:** Athletics	**No. 9:** Pacific Coast	
1987		**No. 3:** Athletics		

YADIER MOLINA, C

BIOGRAPHY

PROPER NAME: Yadier Benjamin Molina. **BORN:** July 13, 1982 in Bayamon, Puerto Rico.
HT: 5-11. **WT:** 205. **BATS:** R. **THROWS:** R. **SCHOOL:** Maestro Ladi HS, Vega Alta, Puerto Rico.
FIRST PRO CONTRACT: Selected by Cardinals in fourth round (113th overall) of 2000 draft;
signed Sept. 6, 2000.

ST. LOUIS CARDINALS TOP 10 PROSPECTS FOR 2004

As the brother of Angels catchers Bengie and Jose Molina, Molina has terrific catching bloodlines, and he's on his way toward joining them in the majors. Skipping over high Class A, Molina held his own in Double-A in 2003. The only hiccup came when he missed a couple of weeks with a bruised ankle.

As with his brothers, defense is Molina's calling card. He has a plus arm and soft hands, and led Southern League regulars by throwing out 40 percent of basestealers. He also is advanced for his age in working with pitchers and likes to take charge on the field.

Speed is by far Molina's weakest tool, rating as low as 20 on the 20-80 scouting scale. It hurts him on offense, though he showed progress otherwise in 2003, staying on balls well and going the other way. He needs to do that more consistently and to improve his plate discipline. He never has hit for much power.

Molina was batting third in the Tennessee order by the end of the season. He isn't expected to bat there as a big leaguer, but showed he can handle the bat and continue to move quickly. He'll get a chance to be the starting catcher at Triple-A Memphis in 2004.

— By Will Lingo

MINOR LEAGUE MENTIONS BY BA

YEAR	TOP 100	ORG RANKING	LEAGUE RANKING	BEST TOOLS
2002		**No. 7:** Cardinals		
2003		**No. 10:** Cardinals		
2004		**No. 4:** Cardinals	**No. 10:** Pacific Coast	**PCL:** Best Defensive C

MIKE MUSSINA, RHP

BIOGRAPHY

PROPER NAME: Michael Cole Mussina. **BORN:** December 8, 1968 in Williamsport, Pa.
HT: 6-2. **WT:** 190. **BATS:** L. **THROWS:** R. **SCHOOL:** Stanford.
FIRST PRO CONTRACT: Selected by Orioles in first round (20th overall) of 1990 draft;
signed July 28, 1990.

EASTERN LEAGUE TOP 10 PROSPECTS FOR 1990

Mussina was Baltimore's first-round pick this summer and began his pro career in Double-A. In his debut, he pitched four shutout innings versus Cleveland's John Farrell, who was on rehab at Canton, before 6,700 fans.

"He's very aggressive," (Albany-Colonie manager Dan) Radison said. "His breaking ball is what makes him above-average. His knuckle-curve has bite and good drop."

Mussina went up to Triple-A Rochester the last week of the season. His final numbers at Hagerstown were 3-0, 1.49 in seven starts.

— By Phil Bowman

BALTIMORE ORIOLES TOP 10 PROSPECTS FOR 1991

The Orioles drafted Mussina out of high school in 1987 but couldn't talk him out of a commitment to Stanford. Three years later, Mussina was ready to sign. Working in Double-A and Triple-A last season, he had a 3-0, 1.46 record.

Mussina's next stop might be the Baltimore rotation. He compliments a hard fastball with a curve and a change. Mussina throws a knuckle-curve, but has trouble controlling it.

Like most Stanford products, he works with poise and intelligence. Some time in Triple-A certainly would be worthwhile, but what Mussina lacks probably could be gained with on-the-job training in the major leagues.

— By Ken Leiker

MINOR LEAGUE MENTIONS BY BA

YEAR	TOP 100	ORG RANKING	LEAGUE RANKING	BEST TOOLS
1990			No. 9: Eastern	
1991	No. 19	No. 2: Orioles	No. 3: International	IL: Best Pitching Prospect, Best Breaking Pitch

DAVID ORTIZ, DH

BIOGRAPHY

PROPER NAME: David Americo Ortiz. **BORN:** November 18, 1975 in Santo Domingo, D.R.
HT: 6-3. **WT:** 230. **BATS:** L. **THROWS:** L. **SCHOOL:** Estudia Espillat, Dominican Republic.
FIRST PRO CONTRACT: Signed as international free agent by Mariners, Nov. 28, 1992.

EASTERN LEAGUE TOP 10 PROSPECTS FOR 1997

Size and power always bring comparisons. Ortiz, acquired from the Mariners and formerly known as David Arias, has both size and power, and now he's starting to draw the comparisons. Willie McCovey, Dave Parker and a pre-injury Cliff Floyd. Not bad company.

"He fits in that category," Sweet said. "He shows tremendous power. He doesn't swing at a lot of bad pitches. He needs to work on his defense, but as an offensive player, he's one of the best in the league."

— **By Andrew Linker**

MINNESOTA TWINS TOP 10 PROSPECTS FOR 1998

BACKGROUND: Signed by the Mariners when he went by the last name Arias, Ortiz was acquired by the Twins in September 1996 to complete a deal for Dave Hollins. He was Minnesota's minor league player of the year after starting the year in Class A and finishing in the big leagues.

STRENGTHS: Ortiz is a lefthanded power hitter who should flourish in the Metrodome. He has driven in 223 runs in the last two minor league seasons.

WEAKNESSES: Ortiz will catch what he gets to, but to avoid being a DH he needs to work on his movement. At the plate, he could also be more selective.

FUTURE: The Twins' signing of Orlando Merced should remove the temptation to push Ortiz too fast. He can open the 1998 season at Triple-A Salt Lake.

— **By Tracy Ringolsby**

MINOR LEAGUE MENTIONS BY BA				
YEAR	TOP 100	ORG RANKING	LEAGUE RANKING	BEST TOOLS
1996			No. 6: Midwest	MWL: Best Defensive 1B, Most Exciting Player
1997			No. 6: Eastern	
1998		No. 2: Twins		

ROY OSWALT, RHP

BIOGRAPHY

PROPER NAME: Roy Edward Oswalt. **BORN:** August 29, 1977 in Kosciusko, Miss.
HT: 6-0. **WT:** 190. **BATS:** R. **THROWS:** R. **SCHOOL:** Holmes (Miss.) JC.
FIRST PRO CONTRACT: Selected by Astros in 23rd round (684th overall) of 1996 draft;
signed May 18, 1997.

HOUSTON ASTROS TOP 10 PROSPECTS FOR 1999

BACKGROUND: Drafted out of a rural Mississippi high school, Oswalt signed for $500,000 as a draft-and-follow after a year in junior college. He was scheduled to pitch at Class A Quad City last season but sprained his elbow in spring training. The Astros chose to rehab the injury conservatively and kept him in extended spring.

STRENGTHS: Despite his slender frame, Oswalt has nasty raw stuff. His fastball is regularly in the 93-95 mph range and has touched 97. His curveball has the potential to become a plus major league pitch and the top breaking ball in the system. He has walked 54 hitters in 164 professional innings, impressive for a power pitcher.

WEAKNESSES: Durability is the first hurdle Oswalt has to clear. As he begins to build up innings, he needs to develop a changeup and spot his pitches better within the strike zone.

FUTURE: The Astros will start Oswalt in Class A ball in 1999, but with his plus pitches and mature fundamentals, he has the potential to move quickly.

— **By David Rawnsley**

MINOR LEAGUE MENTIONS BY BA

YEAR	TOP 100	ORG RANKING	LEAGUE RANKING	BEST TOOLS
1999		**No. 9:** Astros		
2000			**No. 3:** Florida State **No. 1:** Texas	**TL:** Best Control
2001	No. 13	**No. 1:** Astros		

JAKE PEAVY, RHP

BIOGRAPHY

PROPER NAME: Jacob Edward Peavy. **BORN:** May 31, 1981 in Mobile, Ala.
HT: 6-1. **WT:** 195. **BATS:** R. **THROWS:** R. **SCHOOL:** St. Paul's Episcopal HS, Mobile, Ala.
FIRST PRO CONTRACT: Selected by Padres in 15th round (472nd overall) of 1999 draft;
signed June 9, 1999.

SAN DIEGO PADRES TOP 10 PROSPECTS FOR 2002

Peavy was running neck and neck with Gerik Baxter and Mike Bynum as the best prospect from San Diego's 1999 draft class, but last year Baxter was killed in an auto accident and Bynum regressed.

The only minor league starter who topped Peavy's 12.7 strikeouts per nine innings last year was Minor League Player of the Year Josh Beckett. One veteran Padres scout says Peavy is the closest thing to Greg Maddux he has seen, and Double-A Southern League managers seconded that comparison.

Peavy puts the ball wherever he wants, whenever he wants. He uses a lively low-90s fastball, a slider and a changeup. Peavy sometimes falls into a finesse mode but has enough on his fastball to beat hitters with it. He began to understand this last year. Of his three pitches, his slider needs the most work.

Peavy has a chance to be the rare high school player who makes the major leagues before he has to be added to the 40-man roster. He'll probably open 2002 in Triple- A and could reach Qualcomm Stadium by the end of the year.

— By Jim Callis

MINOR LEAGUE MENTIONS BY BA

YEAR	TOP 100	ORG RANKING	LEAGUE RANKING	BEST TOOLS
1999			**No. 7:** Arizona	
2000			**No. 7:** Midwest	**MWL:** Best Pitching Prospect
2001	No. 40	**No. 2:** Padres	**No. 5:** California	
2002	No. 28	**No. 3:** Padres	**No. 1:** Southern	

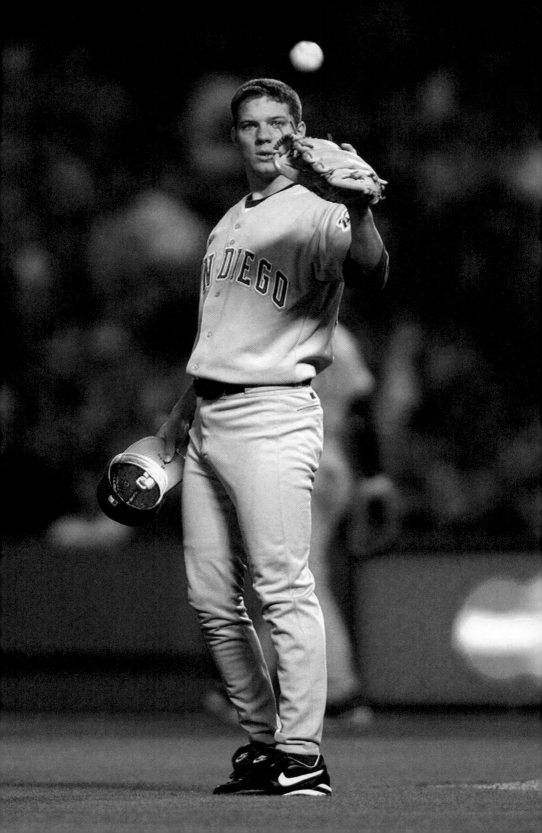

DUSTIN PEDROIA, 2B

BIOGRAPHY

PROPER NAME: Dustin Luis Pedroia. **BORN:** August 17, 1983 in Woodland, Calif.
HT: 5-9. **WT:** 175. **BATS:** R. **THROWS:** R. **SCHOOL:** Arizona State.
FIRST PRO CONTRACT: Selected by Red Sox in second round (65th overall) of 2004 draft;
signed July 21, 2004.

BOSTON RED SOX TOP 10 PROSPECTS FOR 2006

Boston's top pick in 2004, Pedroia was the organization's minor league offensive player of the year in 2005. A wrist injury shortly after a promotion to Triple-A kept him from getting called up to Boston.

He has extraordinary hand-eye coordination. He's able to swing from his heels yet make consistent contact with gap power. Managers rated his strike-zone discipline and second base defense the best in the Eastern League last year. His instincts and makeup are excellent.

Pedroia's arm and range weren't quite up to par at shortstop, though Boston would have kept him there if he hadn't teamed with Hanley Ramirez last year. Pedroia's speed is a step below-average, but he runs the bases well. He needs to get stronger to hold up over a full season.

The Red Sox wouldn't mind giving Pedroia more time in Triple-A. A trade for Mark Loretta, and Tony Graffanino's acceptance of arbitration, probably ended Pedroia's chances of winning the second base job this spring, but there's also a hole at shortstop he might fill.

— By Jim Callis

MINOR LEAGUE MENTIONS BY BA

YEAR	TOP 100	ORG RANKING	LEAGUE RANKING	BEST TOOLS
2005		**No. 6:** Red Sox	**No. 12:** Eastern **No. 17:** International	**EL:** Best Strike-Zone Judgment, Best Defensive 2B
2006	No. 77	**No. 5:** Red Sox	**No. 18:** International	
2007		**No. 7:** Red Sox		

MIKE PIAZZA, C

BIOGRAPHY

PROPER NAME: Michael Joseph Piazza. **BORN:** September 14, 1968 in Norristown, Pa.
HT: 6-3. **WT:** 215. **BATS:** R. **THROWS:** R. **SCHOOL:** Miami-Dade JC.
FIRST PRO CONTRACT: Selected by Dodgers in 62nd round (1,390th overall) of 1988 draft;
signed July 11, 1988.

LOS ANGELES DODGERS TOP 10 PROSPECTS FOR 1993

So much for the science of drafting. The Dodgers waste a decade of first-round picks, and wind up with a 62nd-rounder who reaches the big leagues. Piazza's story is pretty well-known by now. Drafted as a favor to his godfather Tommy Lasorda, the son of a wealthy car dealer worked his way through the farm system with a display of power at all levels and a work ethic that turned him into a decent catcher.

In fact, for all the big offensive numbers he posted last year, management was more impressed with Piazza's improving defense, considering he was a first baseman in school.

He has a strong arm, he's learning to block balls in the dirt and major league pitchers say he handles them well. The Dodgers think so highly of Piazza they didn't mind letting catching fixture Mike Scioscia walk.

For his combination of catching skills and power hitting, Piazza draws favorable comparisons to eight-time All-Star Lance Parrish. That is an irony, in that Parrish has been invited to spring training and could become a combination backup/teacher for Piazza.

What is most impressive about Piazza is that, despite a silver-spoon upbringing and obvious well-placed connections, he works hard for everything. To win the starting job this spring from Carlos Hernandez, Piazza must impress the entire coaching staff. Lasorda says he will avoid charges of nepotism by letting his coaches decide who should start.

— **By Ken Gurnick**

MINOR LEAGUE MENTIONS BY BA

YEAR	TOP 100	ORG RANKING	LEAGUE RANKING	BEST TOOLS
1991				**CAL:** Best Power
1992		**No. 10:** Dodgers	**No. 5:** Pacific Coast	
1993	No. 38	**No. 1:** Dodgers		

Fame, Elvis Connection Mean Little To Kirk Presley
Bonus Section: Baseball Books

Baseball America

ROOKIES! ROOKIES! AND MORE ROOKIES!

MAMA MIA!
MIKE PIAZZA
GOES FROM
THE 62ND ROUND
TO DODGER STADIUM

THE TOP 20

BUSTER POSEY, C

BIOGRAPHY

PROPER NAME: Gerald Dempsey Posey. **BORN:** March 27, 1987 in Leesburg, Ga.
HT: 6-1. **WT:** 210. **BATS:** R. **THROWS:** R. **SCHOOL:** Florida State.
FIRST PRO CONTRACT: Selected by Giants in first round (fifth overall) of 2008 draft;
signed Aug. 15, 2008.

SAN FRANCISCO GIANTS TOP 10 PROSPECTS FOR 2009

Posey led NCAA Division I in hitting (.463), on-base percentage (.566), slugging (.879), hits (119), total bases (226) and RBIs (93) in 2008, en route to winning Baseball America's College Player of the Year and the Golden Spikes awards. The Rays considered him with the first overall pick, but he slid to the Giants at No. 5. He received the largest up-front bonus in draft history, $6.2 million.

There might have been better pure athletes in the draft, but Posey has few peers when it comes to baseball athleticism. He was drafted out of high school as a pitcher and moved from shortstop to catcher at Florida State, where he once played all nine positions in one game. He profiles as a catcher in the mold of Joe Mauer. Posey has a quick bat and makes consistent contact with gap power to all fields. Arm strength isn't a problem, as he hit 94 mph as an occasional reliever for the Seminoles. He's agile and has soft hands, and he even runs well. He's a captain on the field and wins plaudits for his baseball acumen.

Posey is still relatively new to catching and will need time to develop behind the plate, especially his game-calling skills. He had trouble with passed balls in Hawaii Winter Baseball and was sent back to instructional league for a crash course in receiving. Despite his huge power numbers as a college junior, some scouts believe he won't hit more than 10-12 homers annually in the majors. Posey doesn't have to hit for huge power to be an All-Star. He's versatile enough to play anywhere on the diamond, but most valuable as a catcher. He's probably headed for Double-A, where he'll catch a talented pitching staff.

— **By Andy Baggarly**

MINOR LEAGUE MENTIONS BY BA

YEAR	TOP 100	ORG RANKING	LEAGUE RANKING	BEST TOOLS
2009	No. 14	**No. 2:** Giants	**No. 1:** California **No. 1:** Pacific Coast	**CAL:** Best Defensive C
2010	No. 7	**No. 1:** Giants	**No. 1:** Pacific Coast	**PCL:** Best Hitter

DAVID PRICE, LHP

BIOGRAPHY

PROPER NAME: David Taylor Price. **BORN:** August 26, 1985 in Murfreesboro, Tenn.
HT: 6-5. **WT:** 215. **BATS:** L. **THROWS:** L. **SCHOOL:** Vanderbilt.
FIRST PRO CONTRACT: Selected by Devil Rays in first round (first overall) of 2007 draft;
signed Aug. 15, 2007.

TAMPA BAY RAYS TOP 10 PROSPECTS FOR 2008

The Rays pegged Price as the first overall pick in the 2007 draft in October 2006 and he never budged from their plans. Price shattered most of Vanderbilt's pitching records while going 11-1, 2.63 and leading NCAA Division I with 194 strikeouts in 133 innings as a junior. He led the Commodores to their first-ever Southeastern Conference regular-season championship and No. 1 ranking, and he received numerous individual honors, including the Baseball America College Player of the Year and the Golden Spikes awards.

Price is the complete package with outstanding athleticism, stuff and make-up. His fastball has great late life and armside run while sitting in the low 90s and touching 95 mph. He throws a plus-plus slider that reaches 87 mph and has a late, sharp bite. His changeup is also a plus pitch with excellent deception and fade. He uses the entire strike zone and is adept at adding or subtracting velocity with all of his pitches to keep hitters completely baffled.

There's no knock on Price. While he still needs to make the adjustment to pro ball, Tampa Bay doesn't see him having any difficulties after he fared well against competition in the SEC and with Team USA. He spent just two weeks in instructional league before returning to Vanderbilt to work toward his degree, but that shouldn't prevent him from moving rapidly through the system.

He has legitimate No. 1 stuff, and he has a deeper repertoire and more polish than Scott Kazmir. Price likely will break into pro ball at high Class A Vero Beach or Double-A, and he could reach Tampa before the end of the season.

— By Bill Ballew

MINOR LEAGUE MENTIONS BY BA

YEAR	TOP 100	ORG RANKING	LEAGUE RANKING	BEST TOOLS
2008	No. 10	**No. 2:** Rays	**No. 2:** Southern	**SL:** Best Pitching Prospect
2009	No. 2	**No. 1:** Rays		

KIRBY PUCKETT, OF

BIOGRAPHY

PROPER NAME: Kirby Puckett. **BORN:** March 14, 1960.
HT: 5-8. **WT:** 210. **BATS:** R. **THROWS:** R. **SCHOOL:** Triton (Ill.) JC
FIRST PRO CONTRACT: Selected by Twins in first round (third overall) of 1982 January draft.

CALIFORNIA LEAGUE TOP 10 PROSPECTS FOR 1983

Another player in his first full year of pro ball, Puckett gave indications of the offensive talent many scouts and managers believe he has. After starting the year with a 16-game hitting streak, he finished at .314, with nine homers and 97 RBIs.

Puckett has been likened to former major leaguer Jimmy Wynn because of his size (5-8, 175) and strength. Wynn, who played for Houston and Los Angeles, was known as the 'toy cannon.'

The 22-year-old outfielder, who spent a year at Bradley University but was drafted by the Twins in January, 1982 out of Triton College in River Grove, Ill. He signed at the end of Triton's 1982 season and stole 48 bases this year in 59 tries and scored 105 runs to finish second in the league to Donell Nixon.

"He's not very big," said Stockton manager Terry Bevington. "But he's got massive legs. He's really strong, and he can run."

"I think he's capable of hitting 20 home runs if he learns to get the bat head out in front and pulls the ball to left field," Visalia manager Harry Warner said.

In the California League's four-game championship series, Puckett went 9-for-16, scored five runs, drove in two more and was successful on all 10 of his stolen base attempts. California League president Joe Gagliardi specially recognized him before presenting the championship trophy.

— By Danny Knobler

MINOR LEAGUE MENTIONS BY BA

YEAR	TOP 100	ORG RANKING	LEAGUE RANKING	BEST TOOLS
1982			**All-Star:** Appalachian	
1983		**No. 4:** Twins	**No. 5:** California	
1984		**No. 1:** Twins		

ALBERT PUJOLS, 1B

BIOGRAPHY

PROPER NAME: Jose Alberto Pujols. **BORN:** January 16, 1980 in Santo Domingo, D.R.
HT: 6-3. **WT:** 240. **BATS:** R. **THROWS:** R. **SCHOOL:** Maple Woods (Mo.) JC.
FIRST PRO CONTRACT: Selected by Cardinals in 13th round (402nd overall) of 1999 draft;
signed Aug. 17, 1999.

ST. LOUIS CARDINALS TOP 10 PROSPECTS FOR 2001

The Cardinals offered Pujols $10,000 to sign in 1999, so he went to the summer amateur Jayhawk League instead and hit .343-5-17, good enough to earn a bonus close to $60,000. Then he proved to be a bargain, with a monster pro debut in which he was the MVP of the Class A Midwest League and the Pacific Coast League playoffs. He followed up by hitting .323 in the Arizona Fall League.

Pujols started hitting in instructional league just after he signed and hasn't stopped. He uses the whole field and has great strike-zone discipline. He goes the other way well and should add power as he moves up. He's still young, but he has the approach of a veteran. He has a strong arm at third base.

Pujols wasn't a more notable amateur prospect because he was much heavier and didn't move well. He's in good shape now, but the Cardinals aren't sure about his defense. He's passable at third, but he already has played a few games in the outfield and could wind up there.

Pujols must have been sad to see 2000 end. The Cardinals are trying to temper expectations after just one pro season, but he could be in the big leagues by 2002, especially with the void at third base created by the Fernando Tatis trade. He likely will start 2001 at Double-A New Haven.

— **By Will Lingo**

MINOR LEAGUE MENTIONS BY BA

YEAR	TOP 100	ORG RANKING	LEAGUE RANKING	BEST TOOLS
2000				**MWL:** Best Hitter, Best Defensive 3B, Best INF Arm
2001	No. 42	**No. 2:** Cardinals		

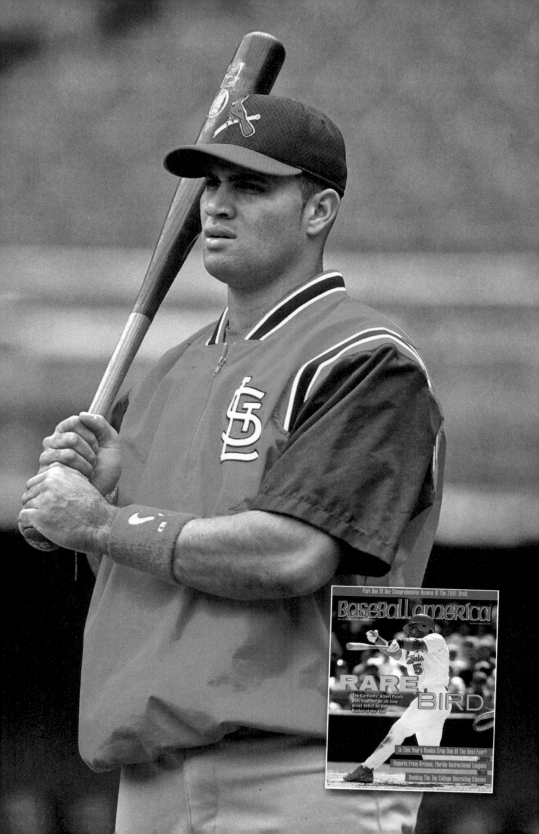

MANNY RAMIREZ, OF

BIOGRAPHY

PROPER NAME: Manny Aristides Ramirez. **BORN:** May 30, 1972 in Santo Domingo, D.R.
HT: 6-0. **WT:** 225. **BATS:** R. **THROWS:** R. **SCHOOL:** Washington HS, New York.
FIRST PRO CONTRACT: Selected by Indians in first round (13th overall) of 1991 draft;
signed June 5, 1991.

CLEVELAND INDIANS TOP 10 PROSPECTS FOR 1993

It's numbers like these that can test an organization's patience: In his two summers of professional baseball, Ramirez, who missed the second half of last season with a hand injury, has gotten 506 at-bats. That's roughly the equivalent of one full season.

His numbers: a .298 average, 32 home runs, 126 RBIs, 29 doubles, eight triples, 96 runs and 79 walks. And Ramirez is just 20.

Though his numbers scream for a fast track to the major leagues, Tribe officials vow not to rush him. The consensus is that it's just a matter of time. The Tribe's first-round pick (13th overall) in the 1991 draft needs only to see some upper-level minor league pitching before rising to the major leagues.

"It's just a matter of him getting experience by playing a little more, and experiencing life as well. Learning to make decisions on his own," said Indians director of baseball operations Dan O'Dowd. "There are no glaring holes in his game."

While Ramirez has hit virtually from day one as a professional, his defense is below average. He has worked hard to improve it. In 1991 he played mostly left field, but as he has matured physically his arm has gotten stronger, and he was moved to right field in instructional league.

— Jim Ingraham

MINOR LEAGUE MENTIONS BY BA

YEAR	TOP 100	ORG RANKING	LEAGUE RANKING	BEST TOOLS
1991			**No. 1:** Appalachian	
1992	No. 37	**No. 3:** Indians	**No. 3:** Carolina	**CAR:** Most Exciting Player
1993	No. 13	**No. 1:** Indians	**No. 2:** Eastern	**EL:** Best Hitter
1994	No. 7	**No. 1:** Indians		

MARIANO RIVERA, RHP

BIOGRAPHY

PROPER NAME: Mariano Rivera. **BORN:** November 29, 1969 in Panama City, Panama.
HT: 6-2. **WT:** 195. **BATS:** R. **THROWS:** R. **SCHOOL:** La Chorrea, Panama City, Panama.
FIRST PRO CONTRACT: Signed as international free agent by Yankees, Feb. 17, 1990.

NEW YORK YANKEES TOP 10 PROSPECTS FOR 1993

Rivera's three-year career has been slowed by injury. He missed the first third of the 1992 season nursing a stiff elbow, made 10 starts, then went down for good and succumbed to elbow surgery. Still, he was placed on the Yankees' 40-man roster.

When healthy, Rivera gives the Yankees plenty to contemplate. He broke into pro ball with a sterling 0.17 ERA in the GCL, and pitched one memorable inning late in the 1992-92 Venezuelan winter season, striking out big leaguers Gus Polidor, Luis Salazar and Andres Galarraga on 10 pitches.

Rivera has increased his velocity on his fastball from 87 to 94 mph since signing, and has excellent command of three pitches. He's scheduled to pitch in Double-A in 1993, elbow permitting.

— **By Allan Simpson**

MINOR LEAGUE MENTIONS BY BA

YEAR	TOP 100	ORG RANKING	LEAGUE RANKING	BEST TOOLS
1993		**No. 9:** Yankees		
1994				
1995		**No. 9:** Yankees		

ALEX RODRIGUEZ, SS

BIOGRAPHY

PROPER NAME: Alexander Enmanuel Rodriguez. **BORN:** July 27, 1975 in New York.
HT: 6-3. **WT:** 230. **BATS:** R. **THROWS:** R. **SCHOOL:** Westminster Christian HS, Miami.
FIRST PRO CONTRACT: Selected by Mariners in first round (first overall) of 1993 draft;
signed Aug. 30, 1993.

SEATTLE MARINERS TOP 10 PROSPECTS FOR 1994

BACKGROUND: Scouts last spring regarded Rodriguez as the best position-player prospect in the draft since Ken Griffey in 1987. The Mariners chose both players with the first pick. Signing Rodriguez became a difficult matter. Agent Scott Boras initially was rejected by the Rodriguez family, but persisted and won favor by promising to deliver a $2.5 million to $3 million deal and by cutting his fee from 5 percent to 2 ½ percent. The Mariners held firm at $1 million. In September, a day before Rodriguez was to attend his first class at the University of Miami and the Mariners were to lose his rights, the club and the family struck a $1.3 million major league deal, much to the chagrin of Boras.

STRENGTHS: Rodriguez is a major league shortstop now. He glides instinctively to the ball and is so quick with his hands it appears he never gets a bad hop. He has exceptional range, especially to his left, and throws with a strong, accurate arm. Rodriguez has the strength and bat speed to hit for a high average and produce 20 homers annually, and he is a slightly above-average runner.

WEAKNESSES: Rodriguez tends to be impatient at the plate and jumps at the ball, which slows his hands. Pitchers in instructional league got him out by pounding fastballs inside, then throwing breaking pitches away.

FUTURE: Assuming he remains with Seattle, Rodriguez will likely begin his pro career at Class A Appleton. He will advance as quickly as his bat allows. Scouts think he could be ready by 1996. Rodriguez needs to mend fences in Seattle, where the organization and fans have been put off by his perceived money-grubbing family and agent.

— **By Ken Leiker**

MINOR LEAGUE MENTIONS BY BA

YEAR	TOP 100	ORG RANKING	LEAGUE RANKING	BEST TOOLS
1994	No. 6	**No. 1:** Mariners	**No. 1:** Midwest	**MWL:** Best Hitter, Best Defensive SS, Best INF Arm, Most Exciting Player
1995	No. 1	**No. 1:** Mariners	**No. 1:** Pacific Coast	**PCL:** Best INF Arm, Most Exciting Player

BaseBall america

ON SALE THROUGH MARCH 20, 1994

TOP 10
PROSPECTS
AL WEST

SEATTLE'S
ALEX
RODRIGUEZ

ANGELS
EXECUTIVE
JACKIE
AUTRY

ODDIBE
McDOWELL
TRIES AGAIN

MARK McGWIRE'S
COMEBACK

AFTER THE HOOPLA
DAVID NIED,
NIGEL WILSON

THE NEW
TV PACKAGE

ESPN'S
Peter Gammons

FRANCISCO RODRIGUEZ, RHP

BIOGRAPHY

PROPER NAME: Francisco Jose Rodriguez. **BORN:** January 7, 1982 in Caracas, Venezuela.
HT: 6-0. **WT:** 195. **BATS:** R. **THROWS:** R. **SCHOOL:** Juan Lovera, Caracas, Venezuela.
FIRST PRO CONTRACT: Signed as international free agent by Angels, Sept. 24, 1998.

ANAHEIM ANGELS TOP 10 PROSPECTS FOR 2001

The Angels ignored Latin America for three years but returned in a big way by signing Rodriguez to a Venezuela-record $900,000 bonus. In his debut a year later, he was the Rookie-level Pioneer League's top prospect. In 121 pro innings, he has allowed just 79 hits and struck out 154.

Rodriguez' fastball is just plain filthy, averaging 94-97 mph and reaching as high as 99 mph, with late life to go with the velocity. His quick arm action makes it look even faster. He throws a slurvy slider from a three-quarters arm angle, and the pitch eats up righthanders. His changeup will be a good third pitch.

Though Rodriguez has a deceptive motion, it's far from pretty and may have contributed to his arm problems in 2000. Shoulder and elbow tendinitis prevented him from making his first start until May 27, and he was shut down for six weeks after three outings because he had a tender forearm. His mechanics have been smoothed out since.

Because Rodriguez is so young and inexperienced, there's no reason to promote him from the high Class A California League to begin 2001. If Joe Torres joins him, they'll form one of the best lefty-righty combos in the minors.

— **By Jim Callis**

MINOR LEAGUE MENTIONS BY BA

YEAR	TOP 100	ORG RANKING	LEAGUE RANKING	BEST TOOLS
1999			**No. 1:** Pioneer	
2000		**No. 2:** Angels		
2001	No. 71	**No. 2:** Angels		
2002		**No. 7:** Angels	**No. 5:** Texas **No. 12:** Pacific Coast	
2003	No. 10	**No. 1:** Angels		

IVAN RODRIGUEZ, C

BIOGRAPHY

PROPER NAME: Ivan Rodriguez. **BORN:** November 30, 1971 in Vega Baja, Puerto Rico.
HT: 5-9. **WT:** 205. **BATS:** R. **THROWS:** R. **SCHOOL:** Lino Padron Rivera, Vega Baja, Puerto Rico.
FIRST PRO CONTRACT: Signed as intertnaional free agent by Rangers, July 27, 1988.

TEXAS RANGERS TOP 10 PROSPECTS FOR 1991

Pudge Rodríguez will play the entire 1991 season as a 19-year-old and already has scouts saying he could hold his own in the big leagues. He's a two-time all-star in the minor leagues and was selected as the No. 1 prospect in the Florida State League by the managers.

Defensively he is at the head of the class, and offensively he has produced at a higher level than the Rangers hoped for in both years. He is only 5-foot-10, but has a solid body that makes him appear bigger. His small stature gives him good mobility behind the plate, where he blocks balls on a big league standard.

There's no question about his arm. Luis Rosa, a scout now with the Chicago Cubs, rates him as a cross between Benito Santiago and Sandy Alomar Jr., two all-star catchers signed by Rosa. He is consistently timed between 1.7 to 1.75 seconds getting the ball to second base, rivaling the arm strength of Santiago. But he does it with mechanics more along the lines of Alomar. There's no toss from the knees or sidearm deliveries.

Despite his youth, Rodríguez shows take-charge ability behind the plate. The Rangers feel they have good young pitching, but Rodríguez is the one who has to handle them and in two years his staffs have finished first and second in their league in ERA. And yes, he is allowed to call his own game.

— By Tracy Ringolsby

MINOR LEAGUE MENTIONS BY BA

YEAR	TOP 100	ORG RANKING	LEAGUE RANKING	BEST TOOLS
1989			**No. 7:** South Atlantic	
1990			**No. 1:** Florida State	**FSL:** Best Defensive C
1991	No. 7	**No. 1:** Rangers	**No. 1:** Texas	**TL:** Best Defensive C

Tim Salmon: Big Fish In The Triple-A All-Star Pond

Olympic Coverage From Barcelona

Baseball america

"BASEBALL NEWS YOU CAN'T GET"

WHAT'S THE CATCH?

MODERN BACKSTOPS FALL
FAR SHORT OF JOHNNY BENCH
AND HIS CONTEMPORARIES,
THOUGH IVAN RODRIGUEZ
OFFERS HOPE FOR THE FUTURE

| BASEBALL'S DRAFT RULE GETS THE THUMB— WHAT'S NEXT? | MAJOR LEAGUE COLUMNISTS ORGANIZATION REPORTS | MINOR LEAGUE COLUMNS NOTEBOOK | ORGANIZATION STATISTICS FOR ALL MINOR LEAGUERS |

JIMMY ROLLINS, SS

BIOGRAPHY

PROPER NAME: James Calvin Rollins. **BORN:** November 27, 1978 in Oakland, Calif.
HT: 5-7. **WT:** 175. **BATS:** B. **THROWS:** R. **SCHOOL:** Encinal HS, Alameda, Calif.
FIRST PRO CONTRACT: Selected by Phillies in second round (46th overall) of 1996 draft;
signed June 24, 1996.

PHILADELPHIA PHILLIES TOP 10 PROSPECTS FOR 2001

Rollins has been among his league's youngest players at every level since coming out of high school in the East Bay, but that hasn't stopped him from turning heads. Rollins continued to exceed expectations by shining in his September callup. He's the cousin of former big league outfielder Tony Tarasco.

Rollins' play belies his stature, as he has improved all facets of his game each year. His batting average, on-base percentage and slugging percentage all have increased steadily in each of the last three seasons. He displays surprising pop from both sides of the plate and puts a lot of pressure on opposing defenses with his quickness. At shortstop, he's a slick fielder with great range in the hole and up the middle, and he possesses the arm strength to make those plays. Rollins has all of the tools to become an exciting leadoff hitter, including bunting skills, basestealing success and bat control. At times, Rollins gets anxious at the plate and chases pitches early in the count. His pitch selection improved during the year and has been solid throughout his career.

The Phillies want him to concentrate on doing the little things atop the lineup, and he'll need to draw a few more walks to be effective in the No. 1 slot. New manager Larry Bowa got his first look at Rollins in the Arizona Fall League and was inspired. Rollins was named to the AFL's all-prospect team, setting the stage for his arrival atop Bowa's first lineup card. He could set the tone for the offense in the same way Rafael Furcal did for Atlanta last year.

— **By Josh Boyd**

MINOR LEAGUE MENTIONS BY BA

YEAR	TOP 100	ORG RANKING	LEAGUE RANKING	BEST TOOLS
1997			**No. 10:** South Atlantic	
1998		**No. 4:** Phillies		
1999		**No. 11:** Phillies		
2000	No. 95	**No. 4:** Phillies		
2001	No. 31	**No. 1:** Phillies		

C.C. SABATHIA, LHP

BIOGRAPHY

PROPER NAME: Carsten Charles Sabathia. **BORN:** July 21, 1980 in Vallejo, Calif.
HT: 6-6. **WT:** 300. **BATS:** L. **THROWS:** L. **SCHOOL:** Vallejo (Calif.) HS.
FIRST PRO CONTRACT: Selected by Indians in first round (20th overall) of 1998 draft;
signed by June 28, 1998.

CLEVELAND INDIANS TOP 10 PROSPECTS FOR 1999

BACKGROUND: It's difficult for Indians officials to decide what they like best about Sabathia: his youth, his size, his arm, or that he's a lefthander. All of those factors combine to make Sabathia perhaps the only untouchable player in the minor league system of a team unafraid to package prospects in trades for veteran help in the big leagues. After getting a late start in 1999 due to a bone bruise in his elbow, Sabathia began galloping up the ladder, pitching at three levels while holding opposing batters to a .198 average.

STRENGTHS: Sabathia is that rarest of commodities: a lefthanded power pitcher. At 18, he was throwing nearly 100 mph. Sabathia has a great feel for pitching for one so young. He has a nice knack for changing speeds, working off a plus fastball. And, despite a somewhat soft body, he is extremely athletic.

WEAKNESSES: Sabathia doesn't exactly have a classic pitcher's body, and because of his body type it will be critical to his success that he works hard to stay in shape. Like most young pitchers he is inconsistent with his breaking ball, and he needs to get a better feel for his changeup. He also needs to get a full season under his belt. A late signee in '98, he has logged just 104 innings.

FUTURE: Still a teenager, Sabathia will begin the 2000 season at Class A Kinston. Indians officials would love to let him get a full season there, but depending on how things develop ahead of him, he may be pushed through the system in much the same way that the club pushed another high school pitcher taken in the first round, Jaret Wright.

— **By Jim Ingraham**

MINOR LEAGUE MENTIONS BY BA

YEAR	TOP 100	ORG RANKING	LEAGUE RANKING	BEST TOOLS
1998			**No. 3:** Appalachian	
1999		**No. 2:** Indians		
2000	No. 57	**No. 1:** Indians	**No. 1:** Carolina **No. 2:** Eastern	**EL:** Best Pitching Prospect, Best Fastball
2001	No. 7	**No. 1:** Indians		

BRET SABERHAGEN, RHP

BIOGRAPHY

PROPER NAME: Bret William Saberhagen. **BORN:** April 11, 1964 in Chicago Heights, Ill.
HT: 6-1. **WT:** 195. **BATS:** R. **THROWS:** R. **SCHOOL:** Grover Cleveland HS, Reseda, Calif.
FIRST PRO CONTRACT: Selected by Royals in 19th round (480th overall) of 1982 draft;
signed July 26, 1982.

FLORIDA STATE LEAGUE TOP 10 PROSPECTS FOR 1983

Another prospect who passed through the FSL on his way to a higher elevation this season, Saberhagen, a former Los Angeles high school standout (Cleveland High), won 10 of his 16 Florida State League starts.

"He has a fine slider to go along with a very fine sinking fastball," noted one observer. And like almost everyone on the Royals' staff, Saberhagen threw strikes (only 19 walks in 110 innings).

His age (19) enhanced Saberhagen's position as one of the league's top prospects. He was promoted to Double-A at Jacksonville (Southern) after compiling a stingy 2.30 ERA.

On a staff that allowed a little more than 2½ walks per contest all season long, Saberhagen's control was perhaps the most impressive. "Especially so," noted one scout, "when you consider he's a little more than a year out of high school."

— **By Joe Sanchez**

MINOR LEAGUE MENTIONS BY BA

YEAR	TOP 100	ORG RANKING	LEAGUE RANKING	BEST TOOLS
1983			No. 5: Florida State	
1984		No. 2: Royals		

CHRIS SALE, LHP

BIOGRAPHY

PROPER NAME: Christopher Allen Sale. **BORN:** March 30, 1989 in Lakeland, Fla.
HT: 6-6. **WT:** 180. **BATS:** L. **THROWS:** L. **SCHOOL:** Florida Gulf Coast.
FIRST PRO CONTRACT: Selected by White Sox in first round (13th overall) of 2010 draft;
signed June 20, 2010.

CHICAGO WHITE SOX TOP 10 PROSPECTS FOR 2011

Sale not only became the first player from the 2010 draft to reach the big leagues, he also finished the season closing games for a contender. The White Sox signed Sale for the slot recommendation of $1.656 million—along with the promise that he'd get every opportunity to race through the minors. He made his big league debut on Aug. 6, faster than any draftee since the Reds' Ryan Wagner in 2003.

Sale has the stuff and lanky build to be a facsimile of future Hall of Famer Randy Johnson, throwing three plus pitches from a low three-quarter delivery. His fastball ranged from 90-95 mph with outstanding late life when he worked as a starter in college, and he averaged 96 mph out of the bullpen in the majors. He hit 100 mph three times in a game against the Royals. Chicago considered his changeup his best pitch when it drafted him—GM Ken Williams compares it to Mark Buehrle's—but he didn't use it much out of the bullpen. Sale used his slider more as a reliever, and it also played up, sitting in the high 80s and topping out at 90. That was important as his slider was questioned coming into the draft. His command is solid, though his arm angle leads to times when he doesn't stay on top of his pitches and leaves them up in the zone.

Sale is unusually poised, capable of making adjustments and pitching out of trouble. Some scouts wonder how durable Sale will be because of his skinny frame, arm action and low slot. He has no history of arm problems, however. Despite his immediate bullpen impact, the White Sox plan to develop Sale as a starter. If he stays healthy, he has the stuff to be a frontline starter or a closer.

— **By Phil Rogers**

MINOR LEAGUE MENTIONS BY BA

YEAR	TOP 100	ORG RANKING	LEAGUE RANKING	BEST TOOLS
2011	No. 20	**No. 1:** White Sox		

JOHAN SANTANA, LHP

BIOGRAPHY

PROPER NAME: Johan Alexander Santana. **BORN:** March 13, 1979 in Tovar, Venezuela.
HT: 6-0. **WT:** 210. **BATS:** L. **THROWS:** L. **SCHOOL:** Liceo Jose Nucete Sardi, Venezuela.
FIRST PRO CONTRACT: Signed as international free agent by Astros, July 2, 1995.

MINNESOTA TWINS TOP 10 PROSPECTS FOR 2000

BACKGROUND: The Twins, with the first pick, acquired Santana in a pre-arranged Rule 5 trade with the Marlins in December. He must make the Twins' Opening Day roster or be offered back to the Astros, his former organization. It might be a longshot for him to stick because he has no experience above the Midwest League.

STRENGTHS: Santana has a loose, live arm and a fastball that ranges anywhere from 88-94 mph. He throws a good curveball with a wide, sweeping break and an advanced changeup for his age. Santana's command of the strike zone and his success in winter ball in Venezuela improve his chances of sticking in Minnesota.

WEAKNESSES: The history of the Rule 5 draft is littered with pitchers who couldn't make the jump from low Class A to the big leagues, or whose careers were harmed by the attempt. Santana must handle the big league environment and the possible inactivity.

FUTURE: Unless Santana fails in spring training, the Twins have committed themselves to carrying him as the third reliever in the bullpen behind Eddie Guardado and Travis Miller.

— **By David Rawnsley**

MINOR LEAGUE MENTIONS BY BA

YEAR	TOP 100	ORG RANKING	LEAGUE RANKING	BEST TOOLS
2000		No. 8: Twins		

BaseBall america

MAJORS • MINORS • PROSPECTS • DRAFT • COLLEGE • HIGH SCHOOL

Twins ace Johan Santana's approach and stuff have made him the most dominant pitcher in the game and our Major League Player of the Year

THE SURE THING

Holiday Gift
Guide: What
The Fan In
Your Life Will
Be Looking For
Under The Tree

Who's At The
Head Of The
Class As We
Hand Out Draft
Report Cards?

At Long Last,
Matt Harrington
Comes To
Organized
Baseball

Billy Beane
Assesses
Oakland's
Season

MAX SCHERZER, RHP

BIOGRAPHY

PROPER NAME: Maxwell M. Scherzer. **BORN:** July 27, 1984 in St. Louis, Mo.
HT: 6-3. **WT:** 215. **BATS:** R. **THROWS:** R. **SCHOOL:** Missouri.
FIRST PRO CONTRACT: Selected by D-backs in first round (11th overall) of 2006 draft;
signed May 31, 2007.

ARIZONA DIAMONDBACKS TOP 10 PROSPECTS FOR 2008

The 11th overall pick in 2006, Scherzer pitched for the independent Fort Worth Cats and held out before he would have re-entered the draft pool. Though he projected as no more than a mid-first-rounder the second time around, Arizona gave him a $3 million bonus, $4.3 million in guaranteed money and another $1.5 million in easily reachable incentives.

Scherzer's fastball can overmatch batters, arriving in the mid-90s with sinking action at its best. His slider also can be a plus pitch, though he's working on its command and plane. Some scouts who saw Scherzer as a starter at midseason wondered what the fuss was about. His fastball sat at 89-93 mph range, and his overall stuff, command, feel and delivery all drew questions. Then they saw him relieving in the Arizona Fall League and he was a different pitcher, touching 98 mph.

Arizona's official opinion is that Scherzer is a starter. If he continues in the rotation, he'll likely open 2008 back in Double-A. If he moves to the bullpen, he could provide immediate help in the big leagues and has the pure stuff to eventually close games.

— **By Will Lingo**

MINOR LEAGUE MENTIONS BY BA

YEAR	TOP 100	ORG RANKING	LEAGUE RANKING	BEST TOOLS
2007			**No. 15:** Southern	
2008	No. 66	**No. 4:** D-backs	**No. 3:** Pacific Coast	

CURT SCHILLING, RHP

BIOGRAPHY

PROPER NAME: Curtis Montague Schilling. **BORN:** November 14, 1966 in Anchorage, Alaska.
HT: 6-5. **WT:** 235. **BATS:** R. **THROWS:** R. **SCHOOL:** Yavapai (Ariz.) JC.
FIRST PRO CONTRACT: Selected by Red Sox in secound round (39th overall) of 1986 January
draft; signed May 30, 1986.

SCHILLING READY, WILLING, ABLE TO LEARN

ROCHESTER, N.Y.—The measure of Curt Schilling's season may have been a 3-2 changeup he threw against the Richmond Braves.

"It was the first time in my life," Schilling, a Rochester righthander, said. "Even up 'til this year, I've always been a power pitcher. I have to mix it up in the count, and I have the confidence to do it."

"Guys get called up and you think, 'Maybe I'm next,'" said Schilling, acquired by the Orioles last season from Boston in the Mike Boddicker trade. "I pretty much feel they planned all the way to leave me here all year … My focus now is to learn and do everything I can for next year."

If the 3-2 change is any indication, Schilling has been a model pupil.

"When we started together this spring, I told him I wanted him to establish some goals," pitching coach Dick Bosman said. "One of the biggest goals was I wanted him to get 200 innings. I knew if you could achieve that goal, a lot of things would take care of themselves."

Schilling pitched 119 innings in 17 starts, and recorded decisions in 15. The 200 innings seems within reach, though Schilling came down with a sore shoulder after his start against Richmond.

— **By Patti Singer**

MINOR LEAGUE MENTIONS BY BA

YEAR	TOP 100	ORG RANKING	LEAGUE RANKING	BEST TOOLS
1990		No. 2: Orioles		

Garrido Helps Texas Hook Its Fifth College World Series Title

Baseball America

MIDSEASON UPDATE

Curt Schilling's all-star season has the Diamondbacks thinking about another playoff run

38

HEAD HEAD

GARY SHEFFIELD, OF

BIOGRAPHY

PROPER NAME: Gary Antonian Sheffield. **BORN:** November 18, 1968 in Tampa.
HT: 6-0. **WT:** 215. **BATS:** R. **THROWS:** R. **SCHOOL:** Hillsborough HS, Tampa.
FIRST PRO CONTRACT: Selected by Brewers in first round (sixth overall) of 1986 draft;
signed June 26, 1986.

MILWAUKEE BREWERS TOP 10 PROSPECTS FOR 1987

BACKGROUND: Five teams passed on him in the first round in June. Mistakes are made. In June 1982, four teams picked before the Mets chose Sheffield's uncle, Dwight Gooden.

STRENGTHS: Sheffield could emerge as quickly as Gooden did. Scouts say he waits on breaking balls better than any high school prospect in recent memory, and he has power to all fields and base-stealing speed. Tearing through the Pioneer and Arizona Instructional leagues last season, Sheffield compiled a .379 average, 18 homers, 97 RBIs and 23 stolen bases in 27 attempts. In 83 games and 314 at-bats, he struck out only 20 times.

WEAKNESSES: While there are no questions about his offense, Sheffield is almost a liability at shortstop. He has the quickness and arm to play the position, but his mechanical work is poor. He doesn't field as much as he reaches and grabs.

FUTURE: Sheffield, who will begin this season at Class A Stockton (California), will have to play himself off shortstop, which is a possibility because his growth is not complete. He probably would go to third base or outfield, although one scout who followed Sheffield closely in high school says he would make a terrific catcher.

— **By Ken Leiker**

MINOR LEAGUE MENTIONS BY BA

YEAR	TOP 100	ORG RANKING	LEAGUE RANKING	BEST TOOLS
1986			**No. 1:** Pioneer	
1987		**No. 1:** Brewers	**No. 1:** California	**CAL:** Best Hitter, Best INF Arm
1988		**No. 1:** Brewers	**No. 2:** Texas **No. 2:** American Association	**TL:** Best Hitter, Best Power
1989		**No. 1:** Brewers		

JOHN SMOLTZ, RHP

BIOGRAPHY

PROPER NAME: John Andrew Smoltz. **BORN:** May 15, 1967 in Warren, Mich.
HT: 6-3. **WT:** 220. **BATS:** R. **THROWS:** R. **SCHOOL:** Waverly HS, Lansing, Mich.
FIRST PRO CONTRACT: Selected by Tigers in 22nd round (574th overall) of 1985 draft;
signed Sept. 22, 1985.

ATLANTA BRAVES TOP 10 PROSPECTS FOR 1988

Don't let his numbers last summer be deceiving. This is a young man with an armful of potential. His command has been a major problem — 123 walks and 133 strikeouts in 244 innings — but the Braves seemed to get that worked out in the instructional league.

Smoltz was a victim of too much advice with the Tigers. Trying to please his instructors, he was trying to throw a variety of breaking balls and change-ups and had not mastered any of them. The Braves finally had him settle down on one breaking ball and one changeup to complement an overpowering fastball. Suddenly, the strike zone does not appear to be the twilight zone.

— **By Tracy Ringolsby**

INTERNATIONAL LEAGUE TOP 10 PROSPECTS FOR 1988

From the way he conducted himself on the mound to his repertoire of pitches, IL managers thought Smoltz was a major league pitcher even before his promotion to Atlanta.

"He has the best combination of fastball and breaking ball for a guy his age I've seen in a long time," said Maine manager George Culver. Even teams that defeated Smoltz wondered how. "He got stronger, threw harder, as the game went along," one manager said.

Add in Smoltz's maturity and Culver sees a winner. "He's growing by leaps and bounds. It's just fun to watch someone pitch with that kind of stuff."

— **By Patti Singer**

MINOR LEAGUE MENTIONS BY BA

YEAR	TOP 100	ORG RANKING	LEAGUE RANKING	BEST TOOLS
1986		**No. 9:** Tigers	**No. 5:** Florida State	
1987		**No. 2:** Tigers	**No. 9:** Eastern	**EL:** Best Fastball
1988		**No. 6:** Braves	**No. 1:** International	**IL:** Best Pitching Prospect, Best Fastball, Best Breaking Pitch
1989		**No. 4:** Braves		

BaseBall america

HOLY
SMOLTZ

DRAFT '96
Early-Round Coverage

Clemson's Kris Benson
Our College Player of the Year

College All-America Team

SAMMY SOSA, OF

BIOGRAPHY

PROPER NAME: Samuel Sosa. **BORN:** November 12, 1968 in San Pedro de Macoris, D.R.
HT: 6-0. **WT:** 225. **BATS:** R. **THROWS:** R. **SCHOOL:** San Pedro de Macoris, Dominican Republic.
FIRST PRO CONTRACT: Signed as international free agent by Rangers, July 30, 1985.

TEXAS RANGERS TOP 10 PROSPECTS FOR 1987

Philadelphia thought it had signed Sosa at the age of 15. They attempted to hide him until he came of age to legally sign a pro contract, but the Phillies scout was fired in the meantime. The Rangers moved in quickly to sign this latest phenom from the Dominican town of San Pedro de Macoris.

Sosa's brief pro career has had its rough spots. After 30 games in the Gulf Coast League last summer, he was hitting only .207. By the end of the season though, he had raised his average to .275 and led the league with 19 doubles.

Offensively, he has the tools to be a total force, combining average with power and base-stealing ability. Defensively, Sosa has a ways to go. He tends to run on his heels and drop fly balls.

— By Tracy Ringolsby

TEXAS LEAGUE TOP 10 PROSPECTS FOR 1989

"I can do it all," Sosa told the Tulsa media before the season. The 20-year-old Dominican backed up that claim, hitting both for average and power, stealing bases and showing an exceptionally strong arm before his promotion to Texas, which later traded him to the White Sox in the Harold Baines deal.

Sosa's shortcoming include the infrequency with which he draws walks and his overaggresiveness on the base paths, but he should still improve in those areas with experience.

— By Ted Bakamjian

MINOR LEAGUE MENTIONS BY BA

YEAR	TOP 100	ORG RANKING	LEAGUE RANKING	BEST TOOLS
1986			No. 4: Gulf Coast	
1987		No. 2: Rangers		
1988		No. 2: Rangers		
1989		No. 2: Rangers	No. 9: Texas	
1990		No. 2: White Sox		

GIANCARLO STANTON, OF

BIOGRAPHY

PROPER NAME: Giancarlo Cruz-Michael Stanton. **BORN:** November 8, 1989 in Panorama, Calif.
HT: 6-6. **WT:** 245. **BATS:** R. **THROWS:** R. **SCHOOL:** Notre Dame HS, Sherman Oaks, Calif.
FIRST PRO CONTRACT: Selected by Marlins in second round (76th overall) of 2007 draft;
signed Aug. 11, 2007.

FLORIDA MARLINS TOP 10 PROSPECTS FOR 2009

Southern California offered Stanton a baseball scholarship and a walk-on opportunity as a receiver/defensive back, while Nevada-Las Vegas wanted him to play football and walk-on in baseball. Instead, the Marlins stole him in the second round of the 2007 draft for $475,000. In his first full pro season, he ranked second in the minors in homers (39) and total bases (286) and fourth in slugging (.611).

While low Class A Greensboro's NewBridge Bank Park is a bandbox, Stanton's homers weren't flukes. He hit 18 on the road and showed regular light-tower power, prompting comparisons to a young Dave Winfield. He has plus speed and runs out every ball, never letting opponents or the score get him off his game. He has a solid-average arm and played well in both center and right field in 2008.

Stanton's strikeout totals remain high, but Florida insists he has no problem with pitch recognition. He has yet to develop basestealing instincts. He worked with Greensboro pitching coach John Duffy to improve his throwing mechanics and get more out of his arm strength.

Even when he could have helped them acquire Manny Ramirez for the stretch drive, the Marlins deemed Stanton strictly off limits. They're already daydreaming about an outfield that includes Cameron Maybin in center and Stanton in right, but the latter probably won't arrive until 2010 at the earliest.

— **By Mike Berardino**

MINOR LEAGUE MENTIONS BY BA

YEAR	TOP 100	ORG RANKING	LEAGUE RANKING	BEST TOOLS
2008		**No. 11:** Marlins	**No. 3:** South Atlantic	**SAL:** Best Power
2009	No. 16	**No. 2:** Marlins	**No. 1:** Florida State **No. 4:** Southern	**FSL:** Best Power **SAL:** Best Power
2010	No. 3	**No. 1:** Marlins	**No. 1:** Southern	**SL:** Best Hitter, Best Power

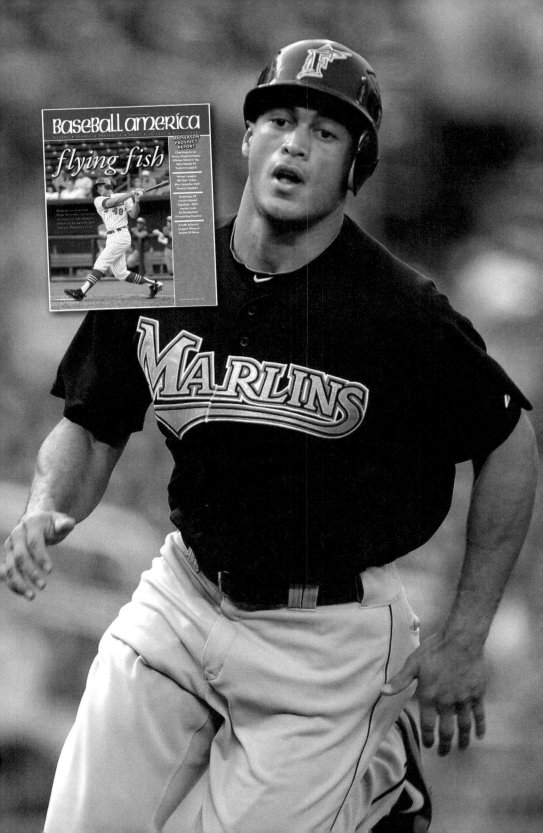

STEPHEN STRASBURG, RHP

BIOGRAPHY

PROPER NAME: Stephen James Strasburg. **BORN:** July 20, 1988 in San Diego.
HT: 6-5. **WT:** 235. **BATS:** R. **THROWS:** R. **SCHOOL:** San Diego State.
FIRST PRO CONTRACT: Selected by Nationals in first round (first overall) of 2009 draft;
signed Aug. 17, 2009.

WASHINGTON NATIONALS TOP 10 PROSPECTS FOR 2010

Strasburg went undrafted out of high school in 2006 because of questions about his conditioning, work ethic and maturity. Three years later, he was the No. 1 pick and regarded by many scouts as the best prospect in draft history.

Strasburg is a once-in-a-generation talent. His plus-plus fastball sits in the mid- to upper 90s and the Nationals have seen him hit 102 mph. His breaking ball rates as a second plus-plus offering, a power 81-84 mph curveball that he can throw for strikes or use as a chase pitch. Even when he doesn't stay on top of it, it's a tough pitch, becoming more of a hard slider. He also flashes a plus changeup, though he seldom needed the pitch to dominate in college. Strasburg has excellent control with all of his pitches, and he also has very advanced command within the strike zone. He's athletic, physical and durable, and he earns raves for his makeup both on and off the field.

The only thing Strasburg doesn't have is pro experience. The general consensus is that there are no red flags in his delivery, as his arm action is fairly loose and he uses his legs well. But it should be noted that there are some within the organization who are concerned that he eventually could break down because he locks out his elbow on his follow through, putting torque on his shoulder.

Strasburg figures to compete for a job in the major league rotation in spring training, and he might never throw a pitch in the minors, though Washington might also choose to ease him into pro ball with an assignment to Double-A or Triple-A. He projects as a true No. 1 starter and a Cy Young Award winner, and anything less will be a disappointment.

— **By Aaron Fitt**

MINOR LEAGUE MENTIONS BY BA

YEAR	TOP 100	ORG RANKING	LEAGUE RANKING	BEST TOOLS
2010	No. 2	**No. 1:** Nationals		

DARRYL STRAWBERRY, OF

BIOGRAPHY

PROPER NAME: Darryl Strawberry. **BORN:** March 12, 1962 in Los Angeles.
HT: 6-6. **WT:** 200. **BATS:** L. **THROWS:** L. **SCHOOL:** Crenshaw HS, Los Angeles.
FIRST PRO CONTRACT: Selected by Mets in first round (first overall) of 1980 draft;
signed July 11, 1980.

TEXAS LEAGUE TOP 10 PROSPECTS FOR 1982

Baseball's No. 1 draft pick by the Mets in 1980, he was voted the Texas League's Most Valuable Player in 1981, and deservedly so. While hitting .283, but spending most of the season hovering around the .300 mark, Strawberry led the league in home runs with 34 and bases on balls with 100. His 97 RBIs ranked third and his 45 stolen bases tied him for second.

At 6-foot-5, and with base-stealing speed, Strawberry can cover the ground in right field. He also has a strong arm, albeit a tad undisciplined. His power is amazing, as he hit some of the longest home runs seen in the league, and he learned in the latter half of the season to take the outside pitch to left field.

The Mets brass keep saying he will be brought along slowly, but the wait is getting shorter. Called up to AAA for the International League playoffs in early September, he was instrumental in leading Tidewater to the Governor's Cup.

— **By Mickey Spagnola**

NEW YORK METS TOP 10 PROSPECTS FOR 1983

He began to feel more comfortable with his role as a future star in New York last summer after batting just .255 with Lynchburg (Carolina) in 1981.

"His skills could allow him to be something awfully special if he continues to develop them," says one Mets' scout.

Strawberry can run, hit with power, has good arm strength and is fast developing into a solid defensive player. There is an outside chance that he could open 1983 in right field for the Mets.

— **By Ron Morris**

MINOR LEAGUE MENTIONS BY BA				
YEAR	TOP 100	ORG RANKING	LEAGUE RANKING	BEST TOOLS
1982			No. 1: Texas	
1983		No. 1: Mets		

ICHIRO SUZUKI, OF

BIOGRAPHY

PROPER NAME: Ichiro Suzuki. **BORN:** Oct 22, 1973 in Kasugai, Japan.
HT: 5-11. **WT:** 175. **BATS:** L. **THROWS:** R. **SCHOOL:** Aikoudai Meiden, Nagoya, Japan.
FIRST PRO CONTRACT: Selected by Orix in fourth round of 1992 Japanese draft; signed by
Mariners, Nov. 30, 2000.

SEATTLE MARINERS TOP 10 PROSPECTS FOR 2001

Known by the single-name moniker of Ichiro in his homeland, he is the seven-time defending batting champion in Japan's Pacific League. He attended spring training with the Mariners in 1999, and when the Orix Blue Wave made him available to major league teams, Seattle bid $13.125 million for the right to sign him, then inked him to a three-year, $22 million deal.

Ichiro has been compared to Wade Boggs and Tony Gwynn as a hitter because he rarely strikes out and uses the entire field. Some scouts believe he'll contend for the American League batting crown right away. He runs well and has the speed and ability to play center field or either of the corners. He owns an accurate arm that plays well, even in right field.

The biggest knock on him has been a lack of power, but like Boggs and Gwynn, he may have the ability to hit for more power at the expense of some batting average.

With Mike Cameron in center, the Mariners will play Ichiro in right field. He should provide a spark from the leadoff spot that the team has lacked for years.

— **By James Bailey**

MINOR LEAGUE MENTIONS BY BA

YEAR	TOP 100	ORG RANKING	LEAGUE RANKING	BEST TOOLS
2001	No. 9	**No. 2:** Mariners		

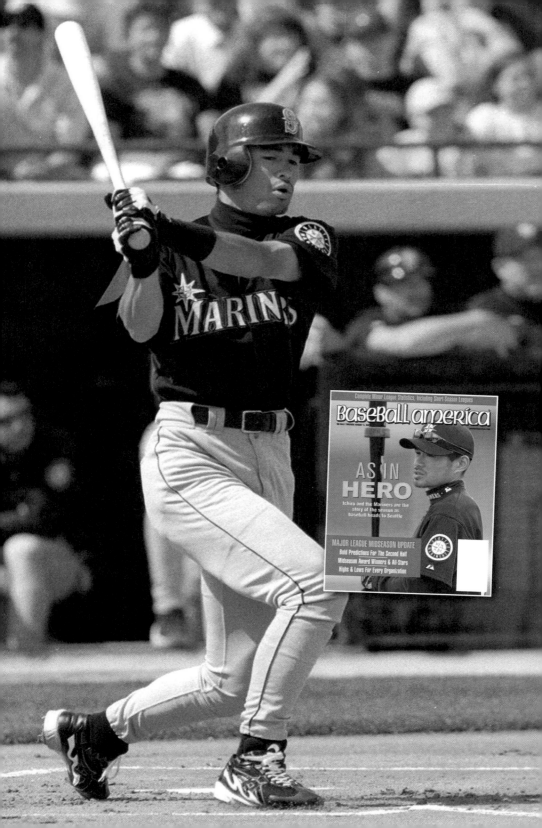

MARK TEIXEIRA, 1B

BIOGRAPHY

PROPER NAME: Mark Charles Teixeira. **BORN:** April 11, 1980 in Annapolis, Md.
HT: 6-3. **WT:** 225. **BATS:** B. **THROWS:** R. **SCHOOL:** Georgia Tech.
FIRST PRO CONTRACT: Selected by Rangers in first round (fifth overall) of 2001 draft;
signed Aug. 24, 2001.

TEXAS RANGERS TOP 10 PROSPECTS FOR 2003

Teixeira had a decorated career at Georgia Tech, where he was Baseball America's College Player of the Year in 2000. His junior season was interrupted by a broken right ankle. The injury, and perceived bonus demands, contributed to him being available to the Rangers with the No. 5 overall pick in 2001.

Teixeira's tools, approach and strength make him the best hitting prospect in the minor leagues. He has well-above-average power—40 homers a year is no stretch—and hitting ability from both sides of the plate, in part because he's in tune with his abilities and has sound fundamentals. Powerfully built, he has a short swing with leverage from both sides, excellent pitch recognition and an advanced two-strike approach. Athletic and instinctive, Teixeira also works hard on the deficiencies in his game.

Teixeira takes pride in not being a base clogger, but speed is his weakest tool. Offensively, he can be stubborn and hasn't taken to the organization's take-a-strike philosophy, but his mindset stems from his success. Teixeira's range at third is average and he had throwing problems in 2002, which the Rangers attribute to injuries and rust. He worked on getting his body back into his throws, and by the Arizona Fall League his arm was again a plus.

His major league ETA depends solely on his health. He figures to start 2003 in Triple-A but should get big league at-bats soon at third base, first base (which he hasn't played since the Cape Cod League in 1999) or DH.

— **By John Manuel**

MINOR LEAGUE MENTIONS BY BA

YEAR	TOP 100	ORG RANKING	LEAGUE RANKING	BEST TOOLS
2002	No. 10	**No. 2:** Rangers	**No. 1:** Florida State **No. 1:** Texas	**FSL:** Best Hitter
2003	No. 1	**No. 1:** Rangers		

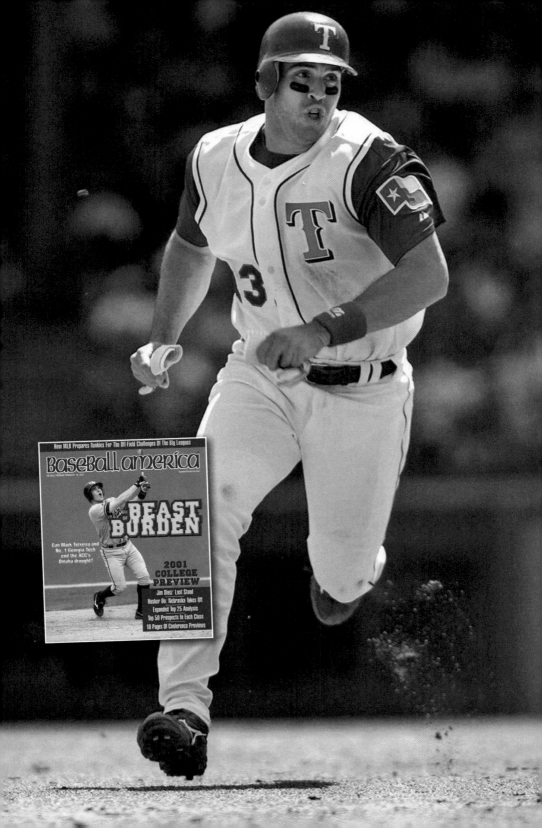

How MLB Prepares Rookies For The Off-Field Challenges Of The Big Leagues

Baseball america

BEAST OF BURDEN

Can Mark Teixeira and No. 1 Georgia Tech end the ACC's Omaha drought?

2001 COLLEGE PREVIEW

Jim Dietz' Last Stand
Husker Do: Nebraska Takes Off
Expanded Top 25 Analysis
Top 50 Prospects In Each Class
10 Pages Of Conference Previews

MIGUEL TEJADA, SS

BIOGRAPHY

PROPER NAME: Miguel Odalis Tejada. **BORN:** May 25, 1974 in Bani, Dominican Republic.
HT: 5-9. **WT:** 220. **BATS:** R. **THROWS:** R. **SCHOOL:** Bani, Dominican Republic.
FIRST PRO CONTRACT: Signed as international free agent by Athletics, July 17, 1993.

OAKLAND ATHLETICS TOP 10 PROSPECTS FOR 1997

BACKGROUND: The diminutive Dominican was voted the No. 1 prospect in the Northwest League in 1995 and California League in 1996. Tejada is the poster boy for the Athletics' rich Latin American program, overseen by Hall of Famer Juan Marichal.

STRENGTHS: Tejada is athletic and exciting. He makes seemingly impossible defensive plays, steals bases and hits home runs. What has most impressed the A's is his ability to make adjustments in at-bats. When pitchers start figuring what it takes to get him out, Tejada figures out what it takes to get a hit.

WEAKNESSES: While Tejada makes remarkable plays, he still has trouble with the mundane. Far too many routine grounders turn into boots. Tejada also must improve his endurance. He simply wore out at the end of the Cal League season.

FUTURE: The Athletics' goal is to have Tejada as their starting shortstop in 1998, though that may be optimistic. He's scheduled to start 1997 at Double-A Huntsville.

— **By Casey Tefertiller**

MINOR LEAGUE MENTIONS BY BA

YEAR	TOP 100	ORG RANKING	LEAGUE RANKING	BEST TOOLS
1995			**No. 1:** Northwest	
1996	No. 88	**No. 6:** Athletics	**No. 1:** California	**CAL:** Most Exciting Player
1997	No. 6	**No. 1:** Athletics	**No. 1:** Southern	**SL:** Best Defensive SS
1998	No. 10	**No. 2:** Athletics		

FRANK THOMAS, 1B

BIOGRAPHY

PROPER NAME: Frank Edward Thomas. **BORN:** May 27, 1968 in Columbus, Ga.
HT: 6-5. **WT:** 240. **BATS:** R. **THROWS:** R. **SCHOOL:** Auburn.
FIRST PRO CONTRACT: Selected by White Sox in first round (seventh overall) of 1989 draft;
signed June 11, 1989.

CHICAGO WHITE SOX TOP 10 PROSPECTS FOR 1990

Thomas was not the best talent available when the White Sox spent the seventh pick of June's draft. They took him because there was not a legitimate power prospect in the system, and he could be a 30-homer man someday. His swing might need to be tightened, but he had little trouble with Class A breaking balls. He is an ox at first base, and likely will wind up a designated hitter.

— By Ken Leiker

SOUTHERN LEAGUE TOP 10 PROSPECTS FOR 1990

Thomas, 22, almost bypassed the league this season. He had a sensational spring and was one of the White Sox's last cuts when they broke camp.

Instead of sulking about being sent down, Thomas went to Birmingham and went to work on league pitchers. His .545 slugging percentage and .476 on-base percentage (on the strength of 112 walks in 109 games) made it easy for the White Sox to bring him up in early August.

"He can hit for average, power and is good at getting on base," Birmingham manager Ken Berry said. "He still needs to work hard on his defense, baserunning and situational play, but those are things that come with experience."

— By Rubin Grant

MINOR LEAGUE MENTIONS BY BA

YEAR	TOP 100	ORG RANKING	LEAGUE RANKING	BEST TOOLS
1989			**No. 3:** Florida State	
1990	No. 29	**No. 7:** White Sox	**No. 1:** Southern	**SL:** Best Hitter, Best Power, Most Exciting Player

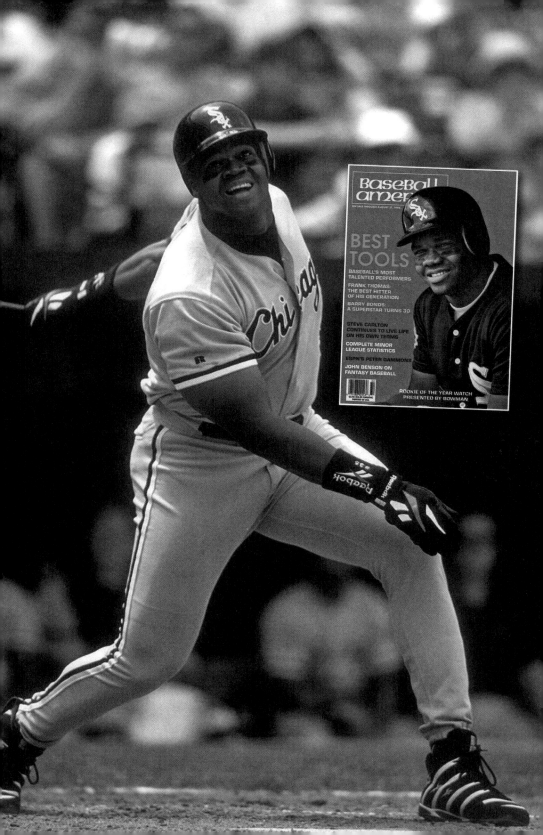

JIM THOME, 1B

BIOGRAPHY

PROPER NAME: James Howard Thome. **BORN:** August 27, 1970 in Peoria, Ill.
HT: 6-4. **WT:** 250. **BATS:** L. **THROWS:** R. **SCHOOL:** Illinois Central JC
FIRST PRO CONTRACT: Selected by Indians in 13th round (333rd overall) of 1989 draft;
signed June 18, 1989.

CLEVELAND INDIANS TOP 10 PROSPECTS FOR 1991

If there is a meteor in the Tribe's farm system, Thome is it. After a mediocre debut in the Gulf Coast League in 1989, he demolished Appalachian League pitching last year, hitting .373-12-34 in 34 games. He was the league's top prospect before being promoted to Class A Kinston, where he hit .308.

By moving closer to the plate and using his hands more, Thome transformed himself from an opposite-field hitter to a more dangerous pull hitter. Rapid maturity between 1989 and 1990 also explains his ascent. He's only adequate defensively, and a position change could be in his future.

— By Jim Ingraham

CLEVELAND INDIANS TOP 10 PROSPECTS FOR 1992

Thome capped a meteoric rise through the system by making his big league debut Sept. 4, just eight days after turning 21. A 13th-round pick in 1989, he simply hit his way to the big leagues, batting .307 in three minor league seasons. He was named the top prospect in the Appalachian League in '90 and No. 1 in the Eastern League in '91.

He held his own in 27 late-season games with the Tribe, showing a strong arm and polished technique coming in on choppers and bunts. He'll go to camp as the favorite to start at third base, but more refining at Triple-A, where he's had only 151 at-bats, may be necessary.

— By Jim Ingraham

MINOR LEAGUE MENTIONS BY BA

YEAR	TOP 100	ORG RANKING	LEAGUE RANKING	BEST TOOLS
1990			**No. 1:** Appalachian	
1991	No. 93	**No. 4:** Indians	**No. 1:** Eastern	**EL:** Best Hitter, Best Defensive 3B
1992	No. 51	**No. 4:** Indians		
1993			**No. 1:** International	**IL:** Best Hitter

MIKE TROUT, OF

BIOGRAPHY

PROPER NAME: Michael Nelson Trout. **BORN:** August 7, 1991 in Millville, N.J.
HT: 6-2. **WT:** 235. **BATS:** R. **THROWS:** R. **SCHOOL:** Millville (N.J.) HS.
FIRST PRO CONTRACT: Drafted by Angels in first round (25th overall) of 2009 draft;
signed July 2, 2009.

LOS ANGELES ANGELS TOP 10 PROSPECTS FOR 2011

After going 25th overall to the Angels and signing for $1.215 million, he ranked as the No. 1 prospect in the Rookie-level Arizona League. Incredibly, Trout was even more spectacular in his full-season followup in 2010. He began the year by hitting .362 at low Class A Cedar Rapids, winning the Midwest League's batting and on-base (.454) titles and MVP award despite getting promoted in mid-July. Managers rated him the best hitter, best and fastest runner, best defensive outfielder and most exciting player in the MWL.

Built like a football defensive back, Trout is a rare five-tool talent who can really hit, a product of his strong, compact stroke and impressive batting eye. He shows no fear of hitting with two strikes, an unusual trait in a teenager. He scores well above-average marks for his running speed—a present and future 80 on the 20-80 scouting scale—and center-field range.

Trout's weakest tools, his power and throwing arm, still grade as average. His physicality and bat speed hint at more power down the road. He handles inside pitches well but has yet to demonstrate that he can pull the ball with consistency. If and when he does, he has the potential to hit 20 or more homers annually. He compensates for fringy arm strength with above-average accuracy.

Like the Braves' Jason Heyward and the Marlins' Mike Stanton in 2010, Trout could be ready to produce in the majors as a 20-year-old come 2012. (He) profiles as a top-third-of-the-order hitter with a wide array of offensive skills and Gold Glove potential on defense.

— **By Matt Eddy**

MINOR LEAGUE MENTIONS BY BA

YEAR	TOP 100	ORG RANKING	LEAGUE RANKING	BEST TOOLS
2009			**No. 1:** Arizona	
2010	No. 85	**No. 3:** Angels	**No. 1:** Midwest **No. 1:** California	**MWL:** Best Hitter, Best Baserunner, Fastest Baserunner, Best Defensive OF, Most Exciting Player
2011	No. 2	**No. 1:** Angels	**No. 1:** Texas	**TL:** Best Hitter, Best Baserunner, Best Defensive OF, Most Exciting Player
2012	No. 3	**No. 1:** Angels		

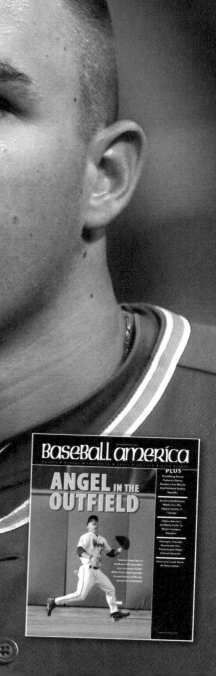

TROY TULOWITZKI, SS

BIOGRAPHY

PROPER NAME: Troy Trevor Tulowitzki. **BORN:** October 10, 1984 in Santa Clara, Calif.
HT: 6-3. **WT:** 205. **BATS:** R. **THROWS:** R. **SCHOOL:** Long Beach State.
FIRST PRO CONTRACT: Selected by Rockies in first round (seventh overall) of 2005 draft;
signed June 10, 2005.

COLORADO ROCKIES TOP 10 PROSPECTS FOR 2007

Tulowitzki was in the big leagues 14 months after he was drafted, the quickest climb of any position player in Rockies history. He's part of an impressive trio of first-round shortstops to come out of Long Beach State this decade, sandwiched between Bobby Crosby and Evan Longoria.

He has legitimate power, but what's most impressive is he understands the need to use the entire field and can drive the ball to right-center as easily as left-center. Tulowtizki spent most of his time in Double-A leading off. The Rockies don't envision him doing that in the majors, but it was a way to have him see more pitches and develop his plate discipline. He has average speed and good baserunning instincts. He'll steal or take an extra base if the opportunity presents itself.

At shortstop, Tulowitzki has one of the strongest and most accurate arms in the game. He has no fear defensively. Most of the work he needs to do center around his defense. Tulowitzki has learned that pure arm strength isn't enough to make difficult plays in the majors, and he's trying to position himself better and get rid of the ball quicker.

Tulowtizki skipped Triple-A and assumed the everyday shortstop job with the Rockies in the final weeks of the regular season. He built off a solid September in the big leagues by being named the top prospect in the Arizona Fall League. Now he's ready to establish himself as a big leaguer for good. Colorado will protect him by initially batting him toward the bottom of the order, but is counting on him evolving into a middle-of-the-lineup run producer.

— By Tracy Ringolsby

MINOR LEAGUE MENTIONS BY BA

YEAR	TOP 100	ORG RANKING	LEAGUE RANKING	BEST TOOLS
2006	No. 25	**No. 2:** Rockies	**No. 3:** Texas	**TL:** Best INF Arm
2007	No. 15	**No. 1:** Rockies		

COLORADO

2

BaseBall america

MAJORS · MINORS · PROSPECTS · DRAFT · COLLEGE · HIGH SCHOOL

PLUS

Tools Of The Trade:
Our Annual Survey
Runs Down Winners
From Major Leagues
Through Full-
Season Minors

Equipment Guide
Gives You Early
Look At Hottest
Gear For Next Year

Sorting Through
Trade Deadline
Rubble

Preview Of Aflac
All-American Classic

Wrapping Up
The Summer For
Team USA

BEST
TOOLS

We sit down and watch tools in action
with a professional scout, and see
just what it is that makes players
like Troy Tulowitzki so good

CHASE UTLEY, 2B

BIOGRAPHY

PROPER NAME: Chase Cameron Utley. **BORN:** December 17, 1978 in Pasadena, Calif.
HT: 6-1. **WT:** 195. **BATS:** L. **THROWS:** R. **SCHOOL:** UCLA.
FIRST PRO CONTRACT: Selected by Phillies in first round (15th overall) of 2000 draft;
signed July 29, 2000.

PHILADELPHIA PHILLIES TOP 10 PROSPECTS FOR 2003

While his Little League teammate Sean Burroughs' move from third base to second failed in 2002, Utley's switch from second to third was successful. He also improved his offensive numbers while making the jump from high Class A to Triple-A.

Utley's sweet line-drive stroke and alley-to-alley power produced an International League-leading 39 doubles last year. He displayed a solid approach and handled breaking pitches well, especially for a player skipping Double-A. He moved closer to the plate and showed the ability to drive the ball hard to the opposite field. Utley's makeup allowed him to handle the position switch and skip a level at the same time.

Utley never was a Gold Glove-caliber second baseman, and he won't win the award at the hot corner either. There are questions about his footwork and arm strength at third base. With hard work, he can be an average defender at either position.

Until the Phillies signed David Bell, Utley was a natural choice to replace Scott Rolen. It's unclear where Utley will play in Triple-A, but he'd make a lot of sense as an offensive second baseman.

— **By Will Kimmey**

MINOR LEAGUE MENTIONS BY BA

YEAR	TOP 100	ORG RANKING	LEAGUE RANKING	BEST TOOLS
2001		**No. 5:** Phillies	**No. 15:** Florida State	
2002		**No. 7:** Phillies	**No. 14:** International	
2003	No. 81	**No. 2:** Phillies	**No. 4:** International	**IL:** Best Hitter

ROBIN VENTURA, 3B

BIOGRAPHY

PROPER NAME: Robin Mark Ventura. **BORN:** July 14, 1967 in Santa Maria, Calif.
HT: 6-1. **WT:** 198. **BATS:** L. **THROWS:** R. **SCHOOL:** Oklahoma State.
FIRST PRO CONTRACT: Selected by White Sox in first round (10th overall) of 1988 draft;
signed Oct. 21, 1988.

1988 COLLEGE BASEBALL PRESEASON ALL-AMERICA TEAM

Robin Ventura is the hitter-supreme of this year's college crops; scouts are unanimous in that assessment. Ventura, in fact, has been likened to four-time AL batting champ Wade Boggs — both in his style of hitting and his approach to it. Like Boggs, he's lefthanded and a line drive hitter who makes contact and uses all of the park.

Scouts even say Ventura is a copycat of Boggs in all other phases of his game — i.e., he's not a particularly good runner and doesn't have good lateral movement at third base. That could hurt his stock in the draft. "He's just a one tool guy," said one scouting director, "and the draft has a history of not taking players high who are hitters only."

Other scouts say the 6-1, 188-pound Ventura has excellent makeup and is willing to work hard at overcoming his deficiencies.

— By Allan Simpson

CHICAGO WHITE SOX TOP 10 PROSPECTS FOR 1990

The hitting machine from Oklahoma State handled Double-A pitching in his first pro season and, despite 27 errors, convinced the White Sox he will be an adequate third baseman. Some scouts say the Sox will have to be satisfied with a line-drive producer because Ventura doesn't have the swing to reach double figures in home runs. The Sox say it's too early to make that judgement.

— By Ken Leiker

MINOR LEAGUE MENTIONS BY BA

YEAR	TOP 100	ORG RANKING	LEAGUE RANKING	BEST TOOLS
1989		**No. 1:** White Sox		**SL:** Best Defensive 3B
1990	No. 15	**No. 3:** White Sox		

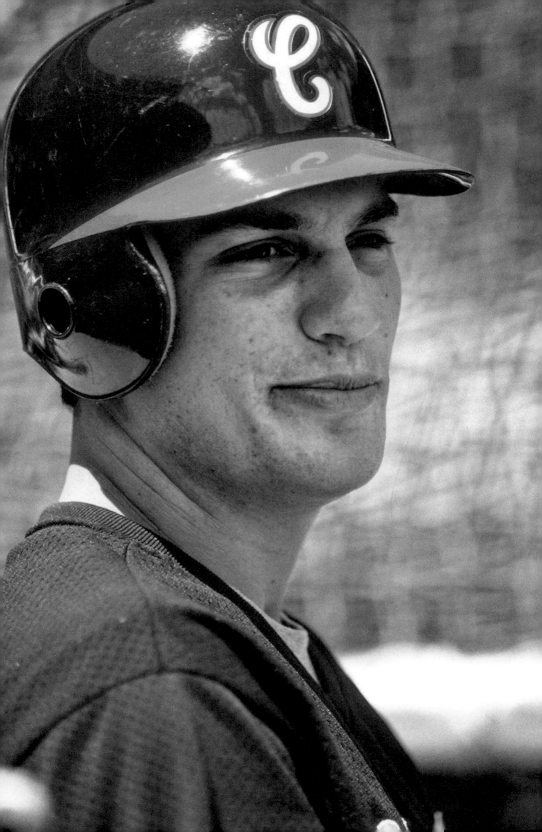

JUSTIN VERLANDER, RHP

BIOGRAPHY

PROPER NAME: Justin Brooks Verlander. **BORN:** February 20, 1983 in Manakin-Sabot, Va.
HT: 6-5. **WT:** 225. **BATS:** R. **THROWS:** R. **SCHOOL:** Old Dominion.
FIRST PRO CONTRACT: Selected by Tigers in first round (second overall) of 2004 draft;
signed Oct. 25, 2004.

DETROIT TIGERS TOP 10 PROSPECTS FOR 2006

The Padres considered Verlander with the No. 1 overall pick in 2004 but he wasn't in their final trio of choices, leaving him available for the Tigers at No. 2. Verlander signed for a $3.12 million bonus and $4.5 million guaranteed major league contract.

Verlander has one of the best arms in the minors and features both the best fastball and curveball in the organization. Tall, lithe and athletic, he generates tremendous arm speed that gives him an electric fastball with both above-average velocity and life. His heater sits at 93-96 mph and touches 99. He commanded his fastball—and all of his pitches, for that matter—much better as a pro than he had in college. Verlander's curveball is a true knee-buckler, a power breaker with excellent depth and late bite down in the zone. He has excellent arm speed on his late-moving changeup, which also improved with his new delivery and ranks among the best in the organization. Stuff-wise, Verlander has no weaknesses. His changeup helped him shackle lefthanded hitters in the minors (.175 average, no homers in 171 at-bats).

The Tigers already have one power righty in their big league rotation in Jeremy Bonderman, who is just four months older than Verlander. He should join Bonderman full-time in the rotation in 2006, if not out of spring training then shortly thereafter. If Verlander learns the nuances of pitching to go with his electric stuff, he could supplant Bonderman as Detroit's No. 1 starter.

— By John Manuel

MINOR LEAGUE MENTIONS BY BA

YEAR	TOP 100	ORG RANKING	LEAGUE RANKING	BEST TOOLS
2005		**No. 3:** Tigers	**No. 2:** Florida State	**FSL:** Best Pitching Prospect, Best Fastball, Best Breaking Pitch, Best Control
2006	No. 8	**No. 1:** Tigers		

**BUMPER
CROP 2**
THE SEQUEL

OMAR VIZQUEL, SS

BIOGRAPHY

PROPER NAME: Omar Enrique Vizquel. **BORN:** April 24, 1967 in Caracas, Venezuela.
HT: 5-9. **WT:** 180. **BATS:** B. **THROWS:** R. **SCHOOL:** Francisco Espejo, Venezuela.
FIRST PRO CONTRACT: Signed as international free agent by Mariners, April 1, 1984.

EASTERN LEAGUE TOP 10 PROSPECTS FOR 1988

Vizquel made the list for his proficiency with the glove, though he showed signs of coming of age with the bat and on the bases. His knowledge of the game belies his age (21). Not only does he have great range and a strong throwing arm, but he played the hitters better than anyone in the league.

"After everyone else has gone in the clubhouse, Omar's out here watching (the opponents) hit," said Vermont manager Rich Morales. "He just sits there and watches and picks up a lot of things that way."

— **By Kevin Iole**

SEATTLE MARINERS TOP 10 PROSPECTS FOR 1989

There's something about Venezuela and shortstops. Vizquel, signed as a free agent in 1984, promises to maintain that tradition. He's a smooth fielder with exceptional range, soft hands and a strong arm coveted by a team that plays on artificial surface.

Only 21, Vizquel hasn't been an offensive force, but he's held his own, and should start to drive the ball as he gets stronger. He at least knows the strike zone (never more than 58 strikeouts in a season). And he has the speed to be a quality basestealer (57 thefts the last two years).

— **By Tracy Ringolsby**

MINOR LEAGUE MENTIONS BY BA

YEAR	TOP 100	ORG RANKING	LEAGUE RANKING	BEST TOOLS
1987				**CAR:** Best Defensive SS
1988		**No. 8:** Mariners	**No. 4:** Eastern	**EL:** Best Defensive SS
1989		**No. 5:** Mariners		

JOEY VOTTO, 1B

BIOGRAPHY

PROPER NAME: Joseph Daniel Votto. **BORN:** September 10, 1983 in Toronto.
HT: 6-2. **WT:** 220. **BATS:** L. **THROWS:** R. **SCHOOL:** Richview Collegiate Institute, Toronto.
FIRST PRO CONTRACT: Selected by Reds in second round (44th overall) of 2002 draft;
signed Oct. 25, 2004.

CINCINNATI REDS TOP 10 PROSPECTS FOR 2005

The Yankees had Votto fly in from Canada to work out before the 2002 draft. When the Reds found out, they asked him to work out for them first, and they picked him 44th overall after he put on an impressive display.

Votto has excellent strength, discipline and savvy at the plate, a combination that makes him the best hitter in the system and gives him above-average power potential. He works hitter's counts and has a short, compact swing that he repeats well. His 90 walks ranked fifth in the minors in 2004.

Votto's average bat speed prompted one scout to compare him to Brian Daubach. He can be patient to a fault, passing on pitches he can drive. He's still raw as a baserunner and defender.

While Votto's upside is debatable, scouts agree he's a polished hitter who could rush through the minors. Sean Casey's contract has a club option for 2006, so Votto is a rare Reds prospect who could be pushed. He'll start this year back at high Class A, where he ended 2004.

— **By John Manuel**

MINOR LEAGUE MENTIONS BY BA

YEAR	TOP 100	ORG RANKING	LEAGUE RANKING	BEST TOOLS
2003		**No. 14:** Reds	**No. 10:** Pioneer	
2004		**No. 5:** Reds	**No. 7:** Midwest	
2005		**No. 4:** Reds		
2006		**No. 9:** Reds	**No. 7:** Southern	**SL:** Best Hitter, Best Defensive 1B
2007	No. 43	**No. 3:** Reds	**No. 10:** International	**IL:** Best Hitter, Best Strike-Zone Judgment
2008	No. 44	**No. 3:** Reds		

BILLY WAGNER, LHP

BIOGRAPHY

PROPER NAME: William Edward Wagner. **BORN:** July 25, 1971 in Tannersville, Va.
HT: 5-10. **WT:** 180. **BATS:** L. **THROWS:** L. **SCHOOL:** Ferrum (Va.) College.
FIRST PRO CONTRACT: Selected by the Astros in first round (12th overall) of 1993 draft;
signed June 22, 1993.

HOUSTON ASTROS TOP 10 PROSPECTS FOR 1995

BACKGROUND: Wagner dominated college hitters for three years at the NCAA Division III level, averaging 16.2 strikeouts per nine innings. He has maintained a dizzying strikeout pace since being drafted by Houston with the 12th overall pick in 1993, averaging 10.7 per nine innings while holding opponents to a .205 average. Wagner made his major league debut Sept. 13 against the Mets, retiring the only batter he faced.

STRENGTHS: Wagner's sheer velocity astounds even the most casual observer. Despite a slender frame, his fastball is clocked consistently in the 94-96 mph range, and occasionally reaches 98. The ball explodes out of his hand and simply overpowers hitters. Wagner achieves maximum leverage with a flawless delivery. He has a fluid, effortless arm action and his body is perfectly toned.

WEAKNESSES: Wagner needs work on his complementary pitches. His curveball has a chance to become an above-average second pitch, but he needs to throw it for strikes more consistently. He learned the need for a third pitch when he was roughed up a time or two in Triple-A, and has begun in earnest to develop his changeup.

FUTURE: The Astros had planned to bring along Wagner a step at a time, but he already has exceeded that timetable. He has an excellent chance to break camp with the big league club next spring, but could return to Triple-A if it means preserving his role as a starter. He needs to achieve the last little bit of finesse and consistency to excel against big league hitters.

— **By Allan Simpson**

MINOR LEAGUE MENTIONS BY BA

YEAR	TOP 100	ORG RANKING	LEAGUE RANKING	BEST TOOLS
1994	No. 78	**No. 3:** Astros	**No. 2:** Midwest	**MWL:** Best Pitching Prospect, Best Fastball
1995	No. 17	**No. 2:** Astros	**No. 2:** Texas	**TL:** Best Pitching Prospect, Best Fastball
1996	No. 17	**No. 1:** Astros	**No. 3:** Pacific Coast	**PCL:** Best Pitching Prospect

ADAM WAINWRIGHT, RHP

BIOGRAPHY

PROPER NAME: Adam Parrish Wainwright. **BORN:** August 30, 1981 in Brunswick, Ga.
HT: 6-7. **WT:** 235. **BATS:** R. **THROWS:** R. **SCHOOL:** Glynn Academy, Brunswick, Ga.
FIRST PRO CONTRACT: Selected by Braves in first round (29th overall) of 2000 draft;
signed June 12, 2000.

ST. LOUIS CARDINALS TOP 10 PROSPECTS FOR 2004

Wainwright was the top pitching prospect in a deep Braves organization and provides a needed boost to the Cardinals after being the key player in the J.D. Drew trade. In his first season in Double-A, he overcame five straight losses at midseason to go 5-1, 2.14 in his final seven starts and rank 10th in the Southern League in ERA.

Wainwright has an ideal combination of size, talent and makeup. He started working off his 92-93 mph fastball more often at midseason and the positive results were immediate. He also throws a hard curveball and a solid changeup, and he mixes his pitches and throws strikes well. He has a great work ethic and is one of the most intelligent pitchers in the minors.

Wainwright needs to continue to gain confidence and trust his stuff. He tends to be too fine with his pitches instead of challenging hitters. He also needs to get his body stronger so he'll have better durability throughout the season and late into games.

It was encouraging that Wainwright finished the season stronger than he started. He's still maturing and learning his craft and will continue to do so at Triple-A Memphis in 2004.

— **By Will Lingo**

MINOR LEAGUE MENTIONS BY BA

YEAR	TOP 100	ORG RANKING	LEAGUE RANKING	BEST TOOLS
2001	No. 97	**No. 7:** Braves	**No. 3:** South Atlantic	**SAL:** Best Pitching Prospect
2002	No. 42	**No. 2:** Braves	**No. 3:** Carolina	**CAR:** Best Fastball
2003	No. 18	**No. 1:** Braves	**No. 13:** Southern	
2004	No. 49	**No. 2:** Cardinals		
2005		**No. 2:** Cardinals		
2006		**No. 6:** Cardinals		

LARRY WALKER, OF

BIOGRAPHY

PROPER NAME: Larry Kenneth Robert Walker.
BORN: December 1, 1966 in Maple Ridge, Canada.
HT: 6-3. **WT:** 215. **BATS:** L. **THROWS:** R. **SCHOOL:** Maple Ridge (Canada) HS.
FIRST PRO CONTRACT: Signed as international free agent by Montreal Expos, Nov. 14, 1984.

MONTREAL EXPOS TOP 10 PROSPECTS FOR 1987

A former hockey player from Maple Ridge, British Columbia, Walker was the rage of the system last season (.288-33-90 with 18 steals at Burlington and West Palm Beach). He struck out 144 times, but scouts say he has a textbook swing and makes good contact when he doesn't try to hit the ball 500 feet.

He's not helpless against breaking balls and lefthanded pitching, even though he has played only one and a half years. The next step is finding Walker a position. After trials at first base and third, he has been moved to left field.

— **By Rubin Grant**

MONTREAL EXPOS TOP 10 PROSPECTS FOR 1988

Walker suffered torn ligaments in his right knee during the winter season in Mexico and will miss the 1988 season. The damage was severe, but doctors are optimistic that he will recover completely.

Walker is the best Canadian-born prospect in Expos history. He has a flawless lefthanded swing, generates above-average power, runs well and was adapting quickly to the outfield. The Expos shifted him from third base to left field last season and planned to play him in center field at Triple-A this year.

Walker still gives away too many at-bats (264 strikeouts the past two seasons), but scouts say his concentration tightens with runners on base.

— **By Ken Leiker**

MINOR LEAGUE MENTIONS BY BA

YEAR	TOP 100	ORG RANKING	LEAGUE RANKING	BEST TOOLS
1986			**No. 2:** Midwest	**MWL:** Best Hitter, Best Power
1987	**No. 9:** Expos		**No. 3:** Southern	
1988	**No. 5:** Expos			
1989	**No. 3:** Expos		**No. 3:** American Association	**AA:** Best OF Arm

JERED WEAVER, RHP

BIOGRAPHY

PROPER NAME: Jered David Weaver. **BORN:** October 4, 1982 in Northridge, Calif.
HT: 6-7. **WT:** 210. **BATS:** R. **THROWS:** R. **SCHOOL:** Long Beach State.
FIRST PRO CONTRACT: Selected by Angels in first round (12th overall) of 2004 draft;
signed May 31, 2005.

LOS ANGELES ANGELS TOP 10 PROSPECTS FOR 2006

Weaver had one of the most dominant college seasons ever in 2004, going 15-1, 1.63 with 213 strikeouts in 144 innings to win Baseball America's College Player of the Year award. The top-rated prospect for the 2004 draft, he dropped to the Angels at No. 12 because of concerns about his price tag. Weaver held out until a week before the 2005 draft before agreeing to a $4 million bonus. He reached Double-A in his pro debut and later pitched in the Arizona Fall League and the Olympic regional qualifier. His brother Jeff has won 78 big league games in the last seven seasons.

Weaver owns the system's best combination of present stuff and command. His arm is loose and fast, and he works from a three-quarters arm slot slightly higher than that of his brother. He relies on a nasty 86-90 mph two-seam fastball, a 91-93 mph four-seamer, a slider and a changeup. He pitches with tenacity and passion. Weaver's command is more notable than his stuff, and some scouts think he's more of a No. 3 starter than a headliner.

He's an extreme flyball pitcher and is vulnerable to homers. His slider grades as an above-average pitch at times but lack consistency. A free spirit, he loses his cool at times.

Some hyperbolic scouting reports declared Weaver as big league-ready when he entered pro ball, but he is at least another half-season away from joining the Angels. He'll open 2006 in Triple-A.

— **By Alan Matthews**

MINOR LEAGUE MENTIONS BY BA

YEAR	TOP 100	ORG RANKING	LEAGUE RANKING	BEST TOOLS
2006	No. 57	**No. 5:** Angels	**No. 2:** Pacific Coast	**PCL:** Best Pitching Prospect

BaseBall america

MAJORS • MINORS • PROSPECTS • DRAFT • COLLEGE • HIGH SCHOOL

DRAFT PREVIEW

Long Beach State's Jered Weaver thinks and throws his way to the top of the 2004 draft heap

Stanford's Danny Putnam Just Keeps Hitting And Hitting And . . .

Chris Nelson Overcomes Tommy John Surgery To Keep His Draft Stock High

Cowboy Up: Homer Bailey Leads A Pile Of Prep Pitching

Top 100 Draft Prospects, Full Regional Scouting Reports And More

BRANDON WEBB, RHP

BIOGRAPHY

PROPER NAME: Brandon Tyler Webb. **BORN:** May 9, 1979 in Ashland, Ky.
HT: 6-3. **WT:** 230. **BATS:** R. **THROWS:** R. **SCHOOL:** Kentucky.
FIRST PRO CONTRACT: Selected by D-backs in eighth round (249th overall) of 2000 draft;
signed June 6, 2000.

ARIZONA DIAMONDBACKS TOP 10 PROSPECTS FOR 2003

Webb set the Kentucky single-season strikeout record (since broken by Athletics first-rounder Joe Blanton) in 2000, the year Arizona drafted him in the eighth round. After being shut down with a tired arm in his first pro summer, he has been solid ever since. He ranked fourth in the Texas League in both ERA and strikeouts last year.

Webb's fastball tops out at 94-95 mph but is best at 92, where it really sinks. He also has a heavy slider, and his stuff reminds scouts of Bob Wickman's. His two-seam fastball can be so dominant that he could rely on it almost exclusively.

With 40 hit batters and 23 wild pitches over the last two seasons, it's obvious Webb still has work to do to master his command. His pitches have such live, late movement that he can be difficult to catch. He just began to incorporate a changeup into his repertoire last year.

Like his former El Paso teammate Mike Gosling, Webb has an outside chance to make the Diamondbacks roster in 2003. He could be used as either a starter or a long reliever. Whatever the case, he should be a major league mainstay in the near future.

— **By Jack Magruder**

MINOR LEAGUE MENTIONS BY BA

YEAR	TOP 100	ORG RANKING	LEAGUE RANKING	BEST TOOLS
2001		**No. 27:** D-backs		
2002		**No. 26:** D-backs		
2003		**No. 5:** D-backs		

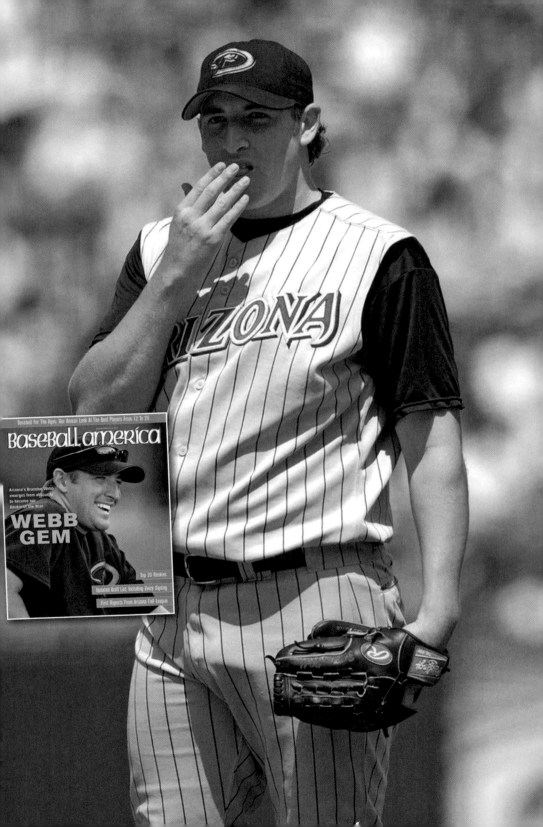

Baseball For The Ages: Our Annual Look At The Best Players From 12 To 25

BaseballAmerica

Arizona's Brandon Webb
emerges from obscurity
to become our
Rookie of the Year

WEBB
GEM

Top 20 Rookies

Updated Draft List, Including Every Signing

First Reports From Arizona Fall League

DAVID WELLS, LHP

BIOGRAPHY

PROPER NAME: David Lee Wells. **BORN:** May 20, 1963 in Torrance, Calif.
HT: 6-3. **WT:** 250. **BATS:** L. **THROWS:** L. **SCHOOL:** Point Loma HS, San Diego.
FIRST PRO CONTRACT: Selected by Blue Jays in second round (30th overall) of 1982 draft;
signed June 18, 1982.

TORONTO BLUE JAYS TOP 10 PROSPECTS FOR 1985

The Blue Jays' second-round pick out of Point Loma High School in San Diego in 1982, Wells would be five or six spots higher if he had a clean bill of health. There are fears he might have to have an operation on his left elbow.

Before the injury, there was no doubt about Wells' future. He is a lefthander with an above-average major league fastball, and he had seemed to find command of the strike zone in 1984.

— By Tracy Ringolsby

TORONTO BLUE JAYS TOP 10 PROSPECTS FOR 1988

The Blue Jays' second-round choice in June 1982, Wells' early years in pro ball were marked by inconsistency and injuries. It was beginning to seem that he would never harness his overpowering fastball and turn it into success.

When the Blue Jays called Wells up a year ago and forced him into their rotation, he was knocked around and sent back to the minors. That's where the major transformation began. The Jays decided to give Wells a whirl as a reliever.

Wells showed the ability to be a dominant short man, and he was Toronto's No. 1 reliever down the stretch, striking out 24 and not allowing a home run in 19 innings during 16 September appearances. He no longer tried to pace himself; he just went in throwing strikes and throwing hard.

— By Tracy Ringolsby

MINOR LEAGUE MENTIONS BY BA

YEAR	TOP 100	ORG RANKING	LEAGUE RANKING	BEST TOOLS
1985		**No. 9:** Blue Jays		
1986				
1987				
1988		**No. 3:** Blue Jays		

DAVID WRIGHT, 3B

BIOGRAPHY

PROPER NAME: David Allen Wright. **BORN:** December 20, 1982 in Norfolk, Va.
HT: 6-0. **WT:** 205. **BATS:** R. **THROWS:** R. **SCHOOL:** Hickory HS, Chesapeake, Va.
FIRST PRO CONTRACT: Selected by Mets in first round (38th overall) of 2001 draft;
signed July 12, 2001.

NEW YORK METS TOP 10 PROSPECTS FOR 2004

Considered one of the best pure hitters in the 2001 draft, Wright quickly showed he also has an advanced knowledge of the strike zone to go with his power potential. Wright led the Florida State League with 56 extra-base hits in 2003, ranking third in slugging percentage and fourth in on-base percentage.

At his best, Wright is a scout's dream. He flashes the potential to be a .300 hitter with 25-30 homers and 80-plus walks. He makes all the plays at third base. He's one of the best in the minors at charging bunts and choppers, and he also shows a major league arm with good accuracy. Wright has average speed and runs the bases well. He responds to instruction well.

In each of his two full pro seasons, Wright has been a streaky hitter. In 2003, he hit .200 through May and June. He works so hard before home games that he wears himself out, and the Mets think he'll be more consistent now that they've gotten him to pace himself.

Wright has steadily moved one level at a time, which should continue in 2004 as he heads to Double-A. He could push for the Mets' third-base job at the end of 2005.

— **By J.J. Cooper**

MINOR LEAGUE MENTIONS BY BA

YEAR	TOP 100	ORG RANKING	LEAGUE RANKING	BEST TOOLS
2001			No. 9: Appalachian	
2002		No. 5: Mets	No. 10: South Atlantic	
2003	No. 75	No. 4: Mets	No. 10: Florida State	FSL: Best Defensive 3B
2004	No. 21	No. 3: Mets	No. 1: Eastern	EL: Best Hitter, Best Strike-Zone Judgment, Best Defensive 3B, Most Exciting Player

BARRY ZITO, LHP

BIOGRAPHY

PROPER NAME: Barry William Zito. **BORN:** May 13, 1978 in Las Vegas.
HT: 6-2. **WT:** 205. **BATS:** L. **THROWS:** L. **SCHOOL:** Southern California.
FIRST PRO CONTRACT: Selected by Athletics in first round (ninth overall) of 1999 draft;
signed June 12, 1999.

OAKLAND ATHLETICS TOP 10 PROSPECTS FOR 2000

BACKGROUND: Even the A's were stunned by Zito's rapid rise. He started his college career at UC Santa Barbara and transferred to Los Angeles Pierce Junior College for 1998 so he could be eligible for the draft. The Rangers picked him in the third round, but Zito didn't sign and went to USC instead, where he had three 16-strikeout starts.

STRENGTHS: Zito is a student of pitching, which helped him rise quickly through the system last year. He displayed his polish with a win in the Triple-A World Series. Zito throws a devastating curveball. His fastball, 89-91 mph with movement, is enough to complement his curve.

WEAKNESSES: Much work remains to develop a satisfactory changeup. Zito still slows his body too much and telegraphs the pitch.

FUTURE: Zito will start the season at Triple-A Sacramento. The A's believe he is close to the majors and could develop into a top-of-the-rotation starter.

— **By Casey Tefertiller**

MINOR LEAGUE MENTIONS BY BA

YEAR	TOP 100	ORG RANKING	LEAGUE RANKING	BEST TOOLS
1999			**No. 4:** California	
2000	No. 41	**No. 2:** Athletics	**No. 2:** Pacific Coast	**PCL:** Best Breaking Pitch

PHOTO CREDITS

Images. BA cover photo by Tom DiPace. **PAGE 135:** Greg Maddux by Focus on Sport/Getty Images. BA cover by Tom DiPace. **PAGE 137:** Russell Martin by Rob Tringali/Sportschrome/Getty Images. BA cover photo by Rick Battle. **PAGE 139:** Edgar Martinez by Ron Vesely/MLB Photos via Getty Images. **PAGE 141:** Pedro Martinez by Focus on Sport/Getty Images. BA cover photo by Steve Babineau/MLB photos. **PAGE 143:** Don Mattingly by Owen C. Shaw/Getty Images. BA cover photo by Tom DiPace (Mass) and Bruce Schwartzman (Mattingly.) **PAGE 145:** Joe Mauer by Larry Goren/Icon SMI/Icon Sport Media via Getty Images. BA cover photo by Linda Cullen. **PAGE 147:** Brian McCann by Brian Bahr/Getty Images. **PAGE 149:** Andrew McCutchen by Ronald C. Modra/Sports Imagery/Getty Images. BA cover photo by George Gojkovich. **PAGE 151:** Jack McDowell by Ron Vesely/MLB Photos via Getty Images. **PAGE 153:** Fred McGriff by Focus on Sport/Getty Images. **PAGE 155:** Mark McGwire by Focus on Sport/Getty Images. BA cover photo courtesy Oakland Athletics. **PAGE 157:** Yadier Molina by George Gojkovich/Getty Images. **PAGE 159:** Mike Mussina by Mitchell Layton/Getty Images. BA cover photo by Ron Vesely. **PAGE 161:** David Ortiz by Sporting News via Getty Images. **PAGE 163:** Roy Oswalt by Mitchell Layton/Getty Images. BA cover photo by Larry Goren. **PAGE 165:** Jake Peavy by Harry How/Getty Images. **PAGE 167:** Dustin Pedroia by Jim McIsaac/Getty Images. **PAGE 169:** Mike Piazza by Ronald C. Modra/Sports Imagery/Getty Images. BA cover photo by Ron Vesely. **PAGE 171:** Buster Posey by Brad Mangin/MLB Photos via Getty Images. BA cover photo by Larry Goren. **PAGE 173:** David Price by Jamie Squire/Getty Images. BA cover photo by Tom DiPace. **PAGE 175:** Kirby Puckett by Focus on Sport/Getty Images. BA cover photo courtesy Minnesota Twins. **PAGE 177:** Albert Pujols by Rich Pilling/MLB Photos via Getty Images. BA cover photo by John Williamson. **PAGE 179:** Manny Ramirez by Focus on Sport/Getty Images. BA cover photo by David L. Greene. **PAGE 181:** Mariano Rivera by Mitchell Layton/Getty Images. **PAGE 183:** Alex Rodriguez by Jonathan Daniel/Getty Images. BA cover photo by Tom DiPace. **PAGE 185:** Francisco Rodriguez by Brian Bahr/Getty Images. BA cover photo by Larry Goren. **PAGE 187:** Ivan Rodriguez by Focus on Sport/Getty Images. BA cover photo by Ron Vesely. **PAGE 189:** Jimmy Rollins by Rick Stewart/Allsport. **PAGE 191:** C. C. Sabathia by David Maxwell/AFP/Getty Images. **PAGE 193:** Bret Saberhagen by Focus on Sport/

Getty Images. **PAGE 195:** Chris Sale by Mark Cunningham/MLB Photos via Getty Images. BA cover photo by Ron Vesley. **PAGE 197:** Johan Santana by Tom Mihalek/AFP/Getty Images. **PAGE 199:** Max Scherzer by Jonathan Willey/Arizona Diamondbacks/MLB Photos via Getty Images. **PAGE 201:** Curt Schilling by Mitchell Layton/Getty Images. **PAGE 203:** Gary Sheffield by Focus on Sport/Getty Images. **PAGE 205:** John Smoltz by Focus on Sport/Getty Images. BA cover photo by Tom DiPace. **PAGE 207:** Sammy Sosa by Focus on Sport/Getty Images. **PAGE 209:** Giancarlo Stanton by Mitchell Layton/Getty Images. BA cover photo by Jerry Hale. **PAGE 211:** Stephen Strasburg by Mark Goldman/Icon SMI/Corbis via Getty Images. BA cover photo by Jesse Soll. **PAGE 213:** Darryl Strawberry by Focus on Sport/Getty Images. **PAGE 215:** Ichiro Suzuki by John G. Mabanglo/AFP/Getty Images. BA cover photo by Larry Goren. **PAGE 217:** Mark Teixeira by John Williamson/MLB Photos via Getty Images. BA cover photo by Robert Gurganus. **PAGE 219:** Miguel Tejada by Jeff Carlick/Allsport. **PAGE 221:** Frank Thomas by Focus on Sport/Getty Images. BA cover photo by Bruce Schwartzman. **PAGE 223:** Jim Thome by Ron Vesely/MLB Photos via Getty Images. **PAGE 225:** Mike Trout by Jeff Gross/Getty Images. BA cover photo by David Stoner. **PAGE 227:** Troy Tulowitzki by Brad Mangin/MLB Photos via Getty Images. BA cover photo by David Stoner. **PAGE 229:** Chase Utley by Al Bello/Getty Images. **PAGE 231:** Robin Ventura by Focus on Sport/Getty Images. **PAGE 233:** Justin Verlander by Mark Cunningham/MLB Photos via Getty Images. BA cover photo by Tom DiPace. **PAGE 235:** Omar Vizquel by Focus on Sport/Getty Images. **PAGE 237:** Joey Votto by Brad Mangin/MLB Photos via Getty Images. **PAGE 239:** Billy Wagner by Sporting News via Getty Images. BA cover photo by Tom DiPace. **PAGE 241:** Adam Wainwright by Matthew Kutz/Sporting News via Getty Images. **PAGE 243:** Larry Walker by Focus on Sport/Getty Images. BA cover photo by Michael Ponzini. **PAGE 245:** Jered Weaver by Stephen Dunn/Getty Images. BA cover photo by Larry Goren. **PAGE 247:** Brandon Webb by Justin Sullivan/Getty Images. BA cover photo by Larry Goren. **PAGE 249:** David Wells by Focus on Sport/Getty Images. **PAGE 251:** David Wright by Brad Mangin/MLB Photos via Getty Images. BA cover photo by David Schofield. **PAGE 253:** Barry Zito by Jed Jacobsohn/Allsport.